ADVANCE PRAISE FOR
Choosing to Be Chosen

"*Choosing to Be Chosen* is an inspiring exploration of what we can become when we listen to the divine rhythm all around us, and how beautiful and satisfying an adventure figuring it out can be. Kylie is a skilled thinker; detailing an awareness that grows and thrives concurrent with her love and her faith. There is something unique and special in Kylie becoming the woman God meant for her to be. This book glows with humility and devotion as well as providing a fresh lens on serendipity and the power that oversees all of our journeys."

—Mayim Bialik, actress

CHOOSING TO BE CHOSEN

CHOOSING TO BE CHOSEN

From Being an Atheist Non-Jew to Becoming an Orthodox Jew

KYLIE ORA LOBELL

A WICKED SON BOOK
An Imprint of Post Hill Press
ISBN: 979-8-89565-348-7
ISBN (eBook): 979-8-89565-349-4

Choosing to Be Chosen:
From Being an Atheist Non-Jew to Becoming an Orthodox Jew

Cover Design by Jim Villaflores

This is a work of nonfiction. All people, locations, events, and situations are portrayed to the best of the author's memory.

Post Hill Press
New York • Nashville
wickedsonbooks.com
posthillpress.com

Published in the United States of America
1 2 3 4 5 6 7 8 9 10

This book is dedicated to the loves of my life, Daniel, Sophia, Ella, and Asher. I am so grateful that Hashem blessed me with all of you.

PROLOGUE

I paced back and forth, refreshing the banking app on my phone to see if any money had come in yet. My rent was due the next day, and I didn't have enough to cover it.

I'd obsessed about it for days at this point. I was unable to concentrate on my work; I couldn't sleep at night. I'd stare up at the ceiling and think, *Why is this happening to me?*

I was so upset at my employers for not paying me on time, at my bank for taking too long to process payments, at myself for getting into this situation in the first place.

I should just quit being a freelance writer, I thought. *I should get a regular job. Who am I to go after my dreams? I keep ending up in the same situation, worrying about my rent every month. I shouldn't live in Los Angeles. It's too expensive. I need to get real about my life. I need to be an adult.*

As I paced, I could only take shallow breaths. My heart was beating too fast.

I looked at my bank account again. Still nothing.

My chest was tightening up.

Why me? Why, why, why? I wanted to scream and cry.

And then, I remembered something I'd once heard from a rabbi.

"God is in control of everything. He has a plan. He knows what's best. Whatever worries you have, hand them over to Him. Do your hard work, put in your effort, and then let God take care of the rest."

I took a deep breath. I was going to forget about my rent being due, put aside my financial problems, and stop beating myself up.

I put my phone in my purse. I looked up at the sky and said, "I'm handing this over to you, God. I trust you."

I couldn't be this anxious person anymore. That was the old me. That was the me before I found God. I didn't want to be stressed out every single day. I wanted to feel at peace with my decisions, with my life.

As I pushed the negative thoughts out of my head and reminded myself to have faith, I felt a wave of calm rush over me.

And then, my phone buzzed. A notification from my bank: My check had come in.

I could pay my rent.

I smiled and said, "Thank you, God."

CHAPTER 1

Ever since Mommy and Daddy got divorced, I'd been spending a lot more time at Grandma Riggle's house.

I didn't like going over there. It was dark. It was cold. And worst of all, Grandma Riggle didn't let me watch cartoons.

"If you want to watch something, I'll turn on Mother Angelica," she'd say.

No, Grandma Riggle, I didn't want to watch an old nun talking about boring stuff from the Bible that I didn't even understand. I wanted to watch *Rugrats* and *Hey Arnold* and jump around your living room like I was Kimberly, the pink Power Ranger.

I couldn't watch my favorite shows or, you know, act like a kid at Grandma Riggle's. Instead, I had to sit down and say the bedtime prayer until I learned it by heart.

"Now I lay me down to sleep, I pray the Lord my soul to keep. If I should die before I wake, I pray the Lord my soul to take."

As I read those scary words, I'd look up at Grandma Riggle's expression. She would be smiling slightly and nodding her head.

"Good," she'd say once I completed it. "We'll do it again next week."

Great.

I thought everything about Grandma Riggle's Catholicism was so frightening, from that bedtime prayer to the pictures of Jesus on the crucifix on her wall, wearing his thorny crown, stark naked, bleeding from his wrists.

I felt like his eyes were watching me.

I learned that as a Catholic, you are born into sin. A friend at school once told me, "If you're not baptized, you're going to hell."

I repeated this to Grandma Riggle.

"Your friend is right," she said, not comforting me at all. "Your parents wouldn't baptize you and your sisters, so I did it in my kitchen sink. It worked for your sisters, but it didn't for you. . . ." Her voice trailed off.

What did that mean? I thought. *Did I smack the water away as it poured down from the faucet?*

After Grandma Riggle told me that, I relayed it to Mommy.

"Don't worry about a baptism," she said, laughing. "You'll be fine."

That didn't reassure me, either.

Aside from the prayers and the baptism talk, Grandma Riggle would sometimes take me to her church. Every year, there was a church carnival, which I loved. I could play games and win prizes and eat as much funnel cake as I wanted.

But then, afterward, she'd make me go to services. I'd sit next to her in the uncomfortable wooden pews, kneeling when she kneeled, not knowing what the priest was saying as I zoned out.

There were no kids my age at church. Everyone was old. I only knew the tunes like "Ave Maria" and "Hail Holy Queen" because of the movie *Sister Act.* And when I wanted to go up and get a cracker and juice—because I was starving by the time we got to that part of the services—Grandma Riggle stopped me.

"You don't get communion," she'd say, putting her hand on mine.

I'd hear the same thing when I was dragged to church on Easter and Christmas. Mommy and my older sisters Rebecca and Christina would come with us, too. When the other people would line up for the cracker and juice, Mommy would whisper to me, "Don't worry, I never got communion either."

Daddy's family wasn't Catholic. They were some other kind of Christian. I don't know if my grandparents on his side, Grandma Jane and Grandpa Bill, ever went to church because we never discussed it. But when I'd say "oh, my God," Daddy would always correct me.

"Don't say that," he'd tell me. "You have to say 'oh, my gosh.' You can't say God's name like that."

I didn't know why; he never explained it to me.

This lack of communication was normal for my family.

Daddy was usually stoic, unless he got mad at me for turning up the thermostat in the winter or, before the divorce, when he and Mommy got into an argument—which happened almost every day toward the end. He didn't smile in photos, rarely gave out hugs, and wouldn't want to talk about his day painting houses. I'd see him get frustrated by the permanent paint stains on his pants, by how hard he had to work to make a living for our family, but he tried to keep it in most of the time.

Mommy, who was a brown-haired, slender-framed beauty, mostly kept to herself, studying her books so she could stop being a housekeeper and become a registered nurse instead. She wouldn't say "I love you" out loud very often, but she'd write it in my birthday and Valentine's Day cards and cuddle me to sleep. Still, I always wanted more attention.

When I was three, I remember taking off my diaper and peeing on her rug just to see if I could get her to stop studying and notice me.

"Mommy, I peed," I said.

"Uh-huh," she said, not looking up from her book.

"I peed on the rug," I said louder, making sure she heard me.

"Yeah, honey," she said, still not lifting her gaze.

I got a towel and wiped up the pee myself.

Before my parents split up, the few times my family and I sat down for dinner together, we would barely talk at the table. I wanted to. I yearned for my parents to ask me about my day. I wanted to tell them about what my friends said at daycare or this new book I was working on at Grandma Jane's house or how I knew all the words to "Skinnamarink," but nobody ever asked. We'd all just sit there, clinking our forks and eating our food until we were done. Then Daddy would go sit in the front of the TV, Mommy would make her way back upstairs to study, and Christina and Rebecca would hang out in their room together or go to their friends' houses.

By the time I was five, I was used to either the silence or the yelling at my house. I didn't know why Mommy and Daddy were so mad at each other or why they couldn't just work it out. I prayed to God every night that they would stay together.

"God," I'd say, tucked into my Winnie the Pooh sheets, "please don't let Mommy and Daddy get divorced."

But they did anyway. I found out one day after school when Rebecca, who was nine at the time, pulled me under the dining room table, put her hands on my shoulders, and looked me in the eyes.

"Tomorrow, we're moving to a brand-new place," she said. "You, me, and Mommy are going to live there."

"What about Daddy?" I asked.

Rebecca didn't answer me. She got up and walked away.

I was confused. I wondered what Rebecca meant. Where were we going?

The next day, while Daddy was at work, Mommy packed up our belongings in the family station wagon. Christina, who was fifteen years old, was going to stay behind with Daddy.

As Mommy, Rebecca, and I walked out the front door, I looked at the empty couch, where I shared some of my best memories with Daddy. Those times when his tough exterior cracked open just a little bit. It's where he'd sit with our Yorkshire Terrier, Corky, and let our dog lick ice cream out of his bowl. We'd watch *Northern Exposure* on the couch together, and during the opening theme song, Daddy would hoist me onto his shoulders and dance around with me. It's where we'd put up the Christmas tree and Mommy and Daddy would sit as my sisters and I excitedly opened up our presents on Christmas morning.

Why wasn't Daddy there to help us move?

Rebecca and I got into the car, and Mommy drove us to our new place, a second-floor walk-up apartment ten minutes from Daddy's. When we got inside, it smelled musty. The carpets were dark brown, and the walls were painted beige. It was small and unfurnished. I looked down and saw little black bugs jumping all over the room.

"Oh, jeez," Mommy said, swatting a bug off her leg. "They didn't bomb the place yet."

Bomb? What did that mean? I imagined a ticking time bomb going off in the apartment and scratched my legs, which suddenly felt intensely itchy.

Mommy ran to the kitchen, found the phone, and made a quick call.

"We need to wait downstairs," she told us.

While Mommy and Rebecca waited in the lobby, I decided to leave. I didn't want to be anywhere near the bugs. I walked outside to the woods next to the building.

At my other house, there were large woods in our backyard. It was where the neighborhood kids and I would walk along the river, skipping rocks and watching the frogs croak. We'd zipline from tree to tree, screaming as we flew. I'd spend hours pretending I was on some great adventure in there.

My new woods were small. There were no neighborhood kids or tall trees. There were no bodies of water or little animals running around. There was no mystery.

I sat on a wet log and waited until Rebecca came out and got me.

"They took care of the fleas," she said. "Come back."

When we got inside, I asked Mommy if Daddy was going to be coming soon.

"No," she said. "We aren't together anymore."

"Am I going to live with you?" I asked.

"Some of the time," she said. "Your father will get you the other half. You'll see him in a few days."

I didn't want to be in this smelly apartment. I wanted to be back at home with Daddy and Mommy and my sisters, even if I had to put up with the fighting and the silent, awkward dinners and everything. I wanted to be anywhere but that apartment.

Why is this happening to me? I thought.

My prayers hadn't worked.

Why couldn't God have kept my parents together? He could do anything, so why couldn't He do that?

I didn't realize it, but my faith had taken a hit that morning when I was carted off to Mommy's new place. And it would be nearly two decades before I got it back.

CHAPTER 2

I tried to see the bright side of my parents' divorce.

I could get double Christmas presents. I wouldn't have to hear Mommy and Daddy fight anymore, which meant they'd hopefully be happier. Mommy's apartment had free HBO and heat, so I could watch movies and crank the thermostat to eighty degrees in the winter if I wanted.

Though I thought I was OK, my body soon told me otherwise.

I was at school when I got sick. It was right after lunch. I was in math class when I suddenly felt ill, and I went to the school nurse's office.

She looked at my tonsils, listened to my heart, and took my temperature, but she couldn't find anything wrong with me, so she sent me back to class. I took two steps out of her office, landed right in front of the principal's office, and threw up all over the floor…and myself.

"Oh, my God," I said, looking at the vomit on my light-up Velcro shoes. I then covered my mouth, Daddy's words echoing in my head: *Don't say God!*

I stood there, frozen and embarrassed. The principal's secretary saw what happened and rushed out to clean me up. She called my mom while I waited back in the nurse's office and changed into some spare clothes she had. They were boys' clothes.

I was sent home in a tight shirt and boys' Ninja Turtles underwear. I was so ashamed. When I got home, I wrapped myself in a blanket and cried. Rebecca found me that way.

"What's wrong?" she asked me.

"I threw up at school, and they put me in boys' underwear," I told her through my tears.

"Aw, don't worry," she said, giving me a hug. "Nobody knows what kind of underwear you had on."

I felt a little bit better in that moment, but a few weeks later, I got sick again. I threw up at my friend's house, and then after going to the zoo with Mommy and Rebecca.

Mommy was concerned, so she took me to my doctor, who touched my stomach all over.

"Do you feel any pain here, Kylie?" he asked.

I looked at Dr. Mullen, an old man with gentle eyes whose glasses rested on the tip of his nose.

"No, I don't," I said.

He took my temperature and looked at my throat and in my ears.

"I see nothing wrong," he said. "You're perfectly healthy."

He paused and lowered his voice.

"Now tell me something, Kylie," he said, sitting down next to me. "Do you think this has to do with your parents not being together anymore?"

I thought about it for a second. I didn't know what he was talking about. Why would the divorce make me have stomachaches and throw up?

"No," I said.

"Uh-huh. Well, OK. If you have any problems, you can always come back to me," he said, putting a smiley face sticker on my shirt and handing me a lollipop.

I was being shuffled back and forth between my parents' houses, since they got joint custody. At Daddy's, I would write in my diary and try to spend time with Rebecca and Christina, but they were usually hanging out at the mall or their friends' houses. When their friends came to our place, I'd try to open the door to their room to hang out with them, but it'd be locked.

"Can I come in?" I'd ask.

"No, go away, we're busy," they'd say. I'd hear them and their friends giggling.

I'd leave the house and see if any of the neighborhood kids were around. If they weren't, I'd ride my bike until the streetlights came on. When Daddy got home from work, he'd heat up some chicken breast and homemade tomato sauce, and I'd sit next to him on the couch as we ate dinner and watched TV. Or I'd go up to my room and eat by myself.

Mommy, who had earned her nursing degree, was working all the time. I became a latchkey kid; when school let out, I'd walk to her house, carrying my heavy Lion King backpack, and let myself in.

I'd open the fridge and see a bag of carrots and some mashed potatoes from the local health food store. In the cabinet, there were always cookies, but that was it. Mommy was very thin, and I was not. I was always hungry. She'd leave me money, and I'd use it to order pizza and french fries and turkey subs to fill myself up. I'd eat until I felt sick.

Going to both of my parents' houses left me feeling lonely. I dreaded being sent to Grandma Riggle's. The only place I truly loved was Grandma Jane and Grandpa Bill's because Grandma Jane was my best friend.

When Mommy and Daddy were fighting before the divorce, I'd call Grandma Jane, and she'd always comfort me.

"Don't worry," she'd say. "Everything will be fine. I'm here for you, sweetie."

Grandma Jane was the only one in the family who said "I love you" out loud. She kissed my cheeks and gave me tight hugs. She kept art supplies in her house so I could create my own children's books.

Grandma Jane, who had silver-colored hair and wore round glasses and silky flower blouses, was the first one to tell me I was a good writer.

"Those are great stories," she'd say. "You've got a real talent there, Kylie. Keep going."

My diary gave me a chance to escape into the page and let out my worries and anxieties. I wrote about how I didn't like my mom's boyfriends, like Rick, who squeezed my hand very hard and made me feel uneasy, or Ralph, the loudmouth guy with slicked-back hair and red cheeks who drove a Mustang with the top down and shushed me in fancy restaurants when I tried to talk. There was also Gordon, who grounded me and locked me in my room, where I felt trapped and cried for him to let me out.

Before Mommy and Daddy's divorce, I didn't feel like I was seen. After, it became so much worse. I felt like a nuisance.

At Grandma Jane's, I never felt that way. She'd asked me what food I wanted her to make and what activities I wanted to do. She would take me to my favorite restaurant, The Ground Round, and order me whatever I wanted. When she picked me up from school, I was always relieved.

She never talked about God, but my family and I would go to her house for Christmas Eve. Those were the best memories I had from my early childhood. Mommy, Daddy, Christina, Rebecca, Grandma Jane, Grandpa Bill, and I would sit around the table, eating delicious foods like roast turkey and mashed potatoes, and then open presents and watch *It's a Wonderful Life* on TV. I'd fall asleep on the car ride home, dreaming about Santa flying in the night sky.

My first Christmas after the divorce looked very different.

Daddy would take us to the woods before Christmas to chop down a tree, but he didn't do it that year. Instead, I came home one day, and it was there—and bare. Christina, Rebecca, and I hung up some lights and decorations and set up our little Christmas village, made of ceramic homes and streetlights and scenes of happy times.

Mommy got a small tree from The Home Depot and decorated it with a few little bulbs. It was nothing compared to our old tree.

That first Christmas, Daddy took us to Grandma Jane and Grandpa Bill's house, but it wasn't the same. We didn't watch any movies, and I stayed up during the car ride home. I looked for Santa in the sky but didn't see him. There was a rumor circulating in my first-grade class that Santa wasn't real; I didn't want to believe it.

I went to Mommy's the next morning, and she had showered me with gifts: a Super Nintendo with all the latest games, a bunch of Barbie dolls, and a new diary. Working as an RN, she made a lot more money now.

"What do you think?" Mommy asked me as I opened my gifts.

"I love them," I said. "Thank you."

"Well, I'm glad. You enjoy them," she said, patting me on the shoulder.

The truth was, I did love my new stuff. I couldn't wait to try it out. But what I really wanted was for my family to be a family again. God couldn't make it happen, and apparently, Santa couldn't either.

CHAPTER 3

Soon enough, I became overweight. I ate too much at Mommy's house and traded for unhealthy snacks at school lunch. The other kids made fun of me.

"You're fat," the boys would taunt me.

"Are you pregnant or is your belly just really big?" one girl said to me.

I had some friends at school who accepted me for who I was. I enjoyed spending time with them during newspaper club, where we made our elementary school paper, *Cougar Tracks*. I'd write little essays about my life and grab the paper as soon as it came out every week just to see my name in print.

The weekends, though, were rough. There was little structure and no one to hang out with. Rebecca and Christina were with their friends or boys—they seemed like they were popular, and it made sense. Unlike me, they were both beautiful and skinny and sociable. I felt awkward, fat, and strange. I didn't know how to easily strike up conversation with people, and I communicated best when I wrote.

I spent a lot of time alone after school and on the weekends, so I didn't get many opportunities to socialize. I'd watch TV and do my homework during the week, and on Saturdays, when my mom worked from 3:00 to 11:00 p.m. at the nursing home, I'd sit at home on the computer, browsing America Online and talking to strangers on instant messenger.

"I'm lonely," I'd tell them. "I feel like I don't have anyone."

"Don't worry, it gets better," my fourteen-year-old online friend Jenny would tell me. "You'll make friends. You'll be happier one day."

By the time I was nine, Mommy decided I was mature enough not to have a babysitter anymore, which meant I'd spend most of the day by myself. I took the time to write, which led me to becoming editor of *Cougar Tracks* by the time I was in the fifth grade.

While I excelled in elementary school at the newspaper and had some friends, middle school was brutal. The bullying got worse because as the other girls matured, I was stuck. I felt like I was still a kid.

I didn't really brush my hair, and Mommy and Daddy didn't care what I wore to school. I dressed myself in oversized, baggy shirts and pants with cartoon characters and Strawberry Shortcake on them. The other girls wore revealing tank tops and sweatpants with the words JUICY or BABY on the back. They knew how to apply shiny lip gloss and bright blue eyeshadow and eyeliner, making themselves look attractive to boys.

I would sit alone on the school bus and wear my headphones, listening to Britney Spears or the Backstreet Boys.

Oftentimes, when I got off the bus, I'd put my hand on my head and there would be spitballs in my hair.

As I pulled them out and held back my tears, I thought: Why wasn't I giggly like the other girls? Why wasn't I obsessed with boys and makeup and passing notes to my friends? And why didn't I stand up for myself?

In my heart, I knew the answer: I thought I deserved the ridicule. I didn't have high self-esteem when it came to anything other than my writing. And God hadn't blessed me in the looks or personality department.

One day, two of the popular girls whom I'd barely talked to—their names were Brittany or Tiffany or something like that—approached me at my locker in between classes.

"Kylie, we heard a rumor that you have a boyfriend. Is it true?" one of them asked. They giggled in synchronicity.

"No," I said.

"Well, you better set the record straight," the other one said. "The whole school saw you kissing a boy."

I was horrified. These girls were making things up about me. Why? What did I do to them?

As they walked away laughing, I hid my head in my locker and cried until the next period.

A few months later, I was in music class when another girl decided to start poking fun at what I was wearing, a shirt that said "Disco Queen" on it.

"Disco Queen? What the hell does that mean?" the girl asked me in front of the class, laughing.

“It just means I like disco,” I said. “It’s like ‘Dancing Queen’ by ABBA. Do you know ‘Dancing Queen’? It’s a really good song.”

“I don’t know who ABBA is, but your shirt is stupid.”

The class laughed, and I was mortified. I sat down in my seat and put my head in my hands.

During these times, I felt like I didn’t have anybody to turn to. I didn’t feel comfortable telling Mommy or Daddy. I didn’t think that Rebecca or Christina would understand, and I didn’t want the few friends I had to think I was a loser.

I certainly didn’t turn to God. After my prayers for my parents to stay together didn’t work, I stopped talking to Him. I didn’t go to Grandma Riggle’s anymore, since I could watch myself, so I didn’t think about religion at all.

Sadly, I couldn’t even rely on Grandma Jane, my closest family member and my best friend, for help.

She was sick.

CHAPTER 4

Grandma Jane had gone from an energetic seventy-six-year-old woman who still lived at home, took care of Grandpa Bill through his chemotherapy treatments, and picked me up from school, to a weak and lethargic version of herself I barely recognized. It only took a few months.

She had colitis. I didn't really understand what it was, but it turned her into someone I didn't recognize. Her cheeks had sunken in, and she'd lost some hair. She could barely talk above a whisper.

She also couldn't get out of the hospital bed, which I found out when I visited her.

On that day, I let Grandma Jane down.

I was there with Rebecca and Christina. As they talked to Grandma Jane about the weather, about school, about birds—her favorite subject—I sat there quietly. I didn't know what to say. I was too shocked by how she sounded and looked. I was scared she was going to die.

I got up in the middle of the conversation to take a break and buy a Coca-Cola from the hospital vending machine.

When I came back and cracked it open, Grandma Jane's eyes lit up.

"Can I have some?" she said faintly.

As I was about to hand it to her, Christina stopped me.

"The doctor said you can't," she said.

"I'm sorry," I said, putting my head down.

Grandma looked so disappointed.

I felt horrible. I wished I had never brought the soda into the room. I wished I could give her some.

A few weeks later, as I was sitting in class, a sound came over the loudspeaker.

"Kylie Wakefield, please report to the guidance counselor's office."

I left class abruptly and went to my guidance counselor, who explained that my mom was picking me up early.

"What's wrong?" I asked.

"Something to do with your grandmother," the counselor said.

When Mommy came to get me, I feared the worst had happened.

"Is everything OK?" I asked her, as we drove away.

"It's not looking good," she said, keeping her eyes on the road. "I think she might pass tonight."

"What?" I said, feeling the tears welling up in my eyes. "What happened?"

"She's not eating. Her breathing is slowing down. The nurses can just tell. I know it'll happen. Probably tonight."

I burst into tears.

"Kylie, it's just how life goes," Mommy said. "People get old, and they have health problems, and they die. Her body is failing her. She wants to go. It's her time. She shouldn't have to be in that dirty hospital anymore."

Because Mommy had worked in a nursing home, she was comfortable around death. She was desensitized, so much so that'd she'd joke about it.

"Wouldn't it be fun if we just put people's dead bodies in wheelchairs and had a party with them after they died?" she'd say. "It would lighten the mood. People shouldn't be so worried about death. When I die, just give my body to science. Don't get a coffin or spend money on a funeral. It's such a waste."

I never knew anyone who died. Mommy's father passed away before I was born.

"He died on a boat," she once told me. "All they found were his teeth that washed ashore."

That story terrified me. I imagined my grandfather was on a large ship that capsized in a storm, and he was thrown into the sea. Then his teeth, which looked like the ones you'd find at the magic shop, washed up onto the beach.

Back in the car, I stared out my window. It had started to rain.

I thought about my memories with Grandma Jane, like that time we spied on the pesky groundhog who was tearing up her garden.

"Let's call him Harry," she said. "Harry the hungry groundhog."

I giggled.

"Hi, Harry! Now go away!" I yelled at him through the window.

I remembered autumn, when Grandma would rake a big pile of vibrant orange and red and yellow leaves I could jump in. I could still feel those beautiful wet leaves on my skin.

I could taste her homemade fudge she made every Christmas and feel her warm embrace when she hugged me.

I cried harder. Mommy kept on driving.

When I walked into Grandma Jane's hospital room, she was lying on her bed, unconscious. Her skin was tinted yellow, and her hands were at her side. I could hear faint daytime television playing in the background and the sound of her heart rate monitor beeping.

I left her room to watch *Maury* in the waiting area with Mommy and Christina and Rebecca. Daddy was in the cafeteria; he'd just arrived from work and was getting some dinner.

I didn't sleep that night, instead going back and forth between the lobby and Grandma Jane's room.

At one point, I clasped my hands together and looked up.

"God," I said, sniffling, "Please let Grandma Jane get better. She can't die. I can't lose her."

As I sat by Grandma's bed, I watched her chest rise and fall. When she took too long between breaths, I got up and made sure she was still breathing.

By the morning, I was so tired that my eyes burned. I slept for a few hours and woke up to the harsh afternoon sun. My sisters and Mommy were there, but Daddy was gone. Mommy told me he went home. He'd been silent since he'd arrived the previous night. As usual, I had no idea what was going through his head.

The afternoon was more of the same: Grandma was still breathing, but she wasn't conscious.

"Is there any chance she'll come back from this?" I asked Mommy.

"It doesn't look like it," Mommy said. "She wants to go."

I was too tired to cry, too tired to think. I zoned out on more of the bad daytime talk shows that the hospital was playing in the waiting room.

Sometime in the late afternoon, I fell asleep again. After what felt like five minutes, I heard Mommy's voice waking me up.

"Come in. It's time," she said, holding me by the arm.

I got up and sat next to Grandma Jane. Her skin had turned a darker shade of yellow. Rebecca and Christina were sitting on the other side of her. We held her hands and put on a CD of bird songs and whispered that we loved her. We cried as her heart rate monitor slowed down, and the little beeps turned into one long beep. At 7:07 p.m., she flatlined.

I cried even harder and held Grandma Jane's hand tight. I thought something would happen, like we'd see her spirit or feel her soul as it went up to heaven. But I saw nothing.

I felt nothing.

After what seemed like more than the three minutes that had passed, Mommy asked my sisters and me, "Do you want to paint her nails?"

I didn't want to. I let go of Grandma's hand. Christina and Rebecca painted Grandma's nails pink before the hospital attendant arrived and wheeled her bed away.

I felt so exhausted. I couldn't believe Grandma Jane was gone.

Mommy turned to us and said, "It's OK. She's not in pain anymore. Death is a natural part of life."

It didn't make me feel better.

I had lost my best friend. How was I going to live without her?

❧

A few days later, we went to Grandma Jane's funeral.

When I saw her, she was wearing bright pink lipstick and blue eye shadow, looking nothing like herself. The mortician had painted over her nails, giving her red ones instead. *What did they do to Grandma?* I thought.

Mommy suggested we take a picture by her open coffin. In the photo, my sisters and I are standing awkwardly side-by-side with solemn looks on our faces.

I didn't know what happened to Grandma now. Was she in heaven? Was there a heaven? Even though I prayed for my parents not to get divorced, they did anyway. Even though I prayed for Grandma Jane not to die, she did.

My prayers didn't work. Or maybe God wasn't listening. Or maybe He didn't care. I didn't know anymore. But I was about to turn my back on Him. I was done.

CHAPTER 5

After school let out for the summer, Mommy sent me to sleep-away camp in rural Maryland. It was there that I met Emily, a rebellious rich girl who smoked cigarettes—even though she was only twelve years old—and hooked up with boys. She was way more mature than I was. I thought she was so cool.

One time, we were talking about life when she casually mentioned to me, “You know, I don’t believe in God.”

“What do you mean?” I asked her.

“God doesn’t exist. Have you ever seen God?”

“No.”

“Then how do you know God exists?”

“I guess I don’t.”

“Right. He’s just like Santa Claus. He’s made up. Something people believe in to give themselves comfort. They’re afraid of death. But me, I’m not afraid of death. I’m a realist.”

I never thought I could just not believe in God. I thought He was real, no questions asked. But now that I had the option to become an atheist, it made sense.

"I don't believe in God either, then," I told Emily. "I'm a realist too."

God didn't answer my prayers. He wasn't there for me. I got bullied, I was shuffled back and forth between my parents' houses, I had a hard time fitting in. If God existed and He was good, then why was my life so crappy?

I decided that the Bible was made up. Those crazy stories about Adam and Eve and Noah's ark were obviously not true. People who believed them were stupid.

The world was a wreck. If God existed, why was the world so messed up? Why did bad people get away with things? Why did good people, like Grandma Jane, suffer?

And what about the so-called "miracles" the Bible proclaimed happened? They just stopped one day? That didn't make any sense. God would have kept the miracles going, right? It was pretty convenient that they just didn't exist anymore.

I was done. Done with believing in God, that fake man in the sky. Faith was for children. Now that I was twelve, I was growing up, and I had to start having adult beliefs. It couldn't have happened at a better time—right when I was going into high school, right when I was finally going to be a teenager, a young adult, and get on with my life. I was going to be mature. I was changing for the better. I was enlightened.

I couldn't wait to see what was in store for me.

CHAPTER 6

My first day of high school felt like a totally different world than what I was used to.

When I walked into the building, I saw students with dyed red and green hair, a girl running down the hallway with a fake tail attached to the back of her T-shirt, and boys and girls carrying cameras and easels covered in paint. It was a stark contrast to my middle school, where everyone looked normal. I could see right away that my high school, Carver Center for the Arts and Technology, was where all the freaks and geeks ended up.

I knew I was home.

Unlike in middle school, I made friends easily. My core group of friends consisted of secular Jewish kids from the Russian and Jewish sides of Baltimore: Owings Mills, Reisterstown, and Pikesville.

There was Sarah, who loved *Friends* and had an infectious laugh. Irina was a Ukrainian immigrant who got me into the band t.A.T.u. Ben was boisterous and sang opera and always had a smile on his face, and Adam wore colorful rainbow beaded bracelets and had lots of gel in his hair. Emma was my best friend; she was always rebelling, shaving all her hair when she got lice and leaving school early to march in anti-Iraq War demonstrations.

We'd spend Friday afternoons at the mall, then go to each other's houses, order pizza, and watch movies. Our parents wouldn't bother us down in the basement.

We'd also go to local punk rock and ska shows at churches and grungy halls. There, I'd throw myself into the mosh pits and crowd surf. I thought about all the bullies from my past, about my parents' divorce, and Grandma Jane's death in those mosh pits. I didn't care if I got hurt. The pain felt good.

I became a punk. I dyed my hair pink and red with Manic Panic temporary hair dye. I wore wear Misfits and Ramones T-shirts and cut them up to make them look grungier. I bought flannel khakis and stuck punk rock patches on them.

One of the patches I got was a classic punk drawing of a stick figure throwing a swastika in the trash; the punk scene was notoriously anti-Nazi. Of course the Nazis sucked, I thought. My friends were Jewish. I had to show how much I hated the Nazis.

I had learned about the Holocaust when I was nine, when Mommy took Rebecca and me to the Holocaust Memorial Museum in D.C. I saw piles and piles of flat black shoes that belonged to the children who were sent to the gas chambers. I learned that the Nazis tortured Jewish people, starving them to death and performing medical experiments on them. As I stood in front of a TV screen in the museum, I saw thousands of emaciated bodies being dumped into ditches. It was the most horrible image I'd ever seen.

I wore my anti-Nazi patch proudly to school until one day, my vice principal, Mrs. Wiggins, took me aside.

"Uh, hi, Kylie," she said.

"Hi, Mrs. Wiggins," I said, gulping.

"Look, I know what your patch means, but maybe some other kids don't. They may get offended, especially if they're Jewish."

"But I'm throwing the swastika *out*, Mrs. Wiggins," I insisted. "It's a good thing! I hate Nazis."

"I know, but maybe consider wearing something else, just in case people get the wrong impression."

I thought about it for a moment. If someone was just walking by and saw just part of my patch, they could get the wrong impression. I didn't want that to happen.

"OK, I will, Mrs. Wiggins," I said, unpinning the patch from my pants. Still, I kept on moshing to the anti-Nazi punk bands I loved.

In the ninth grade, I was happy that I finally felt like I'd found my place at these punk concerts and among my Jewish friends. But at the same time, I was battling crippling depression. It came out of nowhere; one day, I was fine, and the next, I felt I'd be better off dead.

I woke up most days not wanting to get out of bed. I would cry first thing in the morning or in the middle of class and have to run to the bathroom so that no one would see me.

"It's just hormones," Mommy would say when she saw that I was upset. "You'll get over it soon."

Everything was so intense. When I was in a good mood, I felt like I was floating on the clouds. I listened to my music loudly and jumped around. When I was sad, I felt like finding the nearest bridge and jumping off it. There was no middle ground. My mood would swing throughout the day. The smallest thing, like a bad grade, could set me off.

The fact that I wasn't sleeping much compounded the problem. Some nights, I wouldn't sleep one minute, and then I'd go to school the next day. By the time I got home, I felt dizzy. I'd crash for a few hours on the couch while watching TV and stay up all night again.

At times, I was so numb that I just wanted to feel something. In some ways, that was worse.

When that happened, I'd go into my room and sit on my bed with a safety pin in my hand and start slowly scratching my wrists until they bled. Until I cried.

After I'd been doing this for a few months, Mommy saw my scratches.

"What are you doing?" she said, looking at my wrist. "I used to do that. Don't do that. They look like cat scratches."

I hid my wrists under long-sleeve shirts after that and continued to hurt myself.

I had a friend, Lindsay, who was also depressed. She'd always want to hold my hand in homeroom and talk about how messed up her parents were.

She'd bring vodka in orange juice bottles to school, swigging them during first period. Then, she started to steal her parents' pills.

During first period on a Monday morning, she asked me if I wanted some.

"OK," I said, whispering to her from behind my computer, not wanting our teacher to hear me.

She handed me a Ziploc bag of five pills, explaining that they were for anxiety. I didn't know what they were called.

"You owe me twenty bucks, but you can pay me later. Enjoy," Lindsay said with a grin.

I popped one right then and there, washing it down with Coca-Cola, and then whispered to her that I didn't feel anything.

"Well, they're real," she said. "Just you wait."

Just twenty minutes later, I felt lightheaded and happy. I skipped down the halls to biology and sat in the back, alternating between doodling and staring up at the ceiling. My friend Emma, who was sitting behind me, tapped me on the shoulder.

"Did you smoke weed or something?" she whispered.

"No," I said defiantly.

"Then what's going on?" she said, laughing. "You're acting high as a kite."

"Oh, well, Lindsay gave me a pill. I feel great!" I said, a little too loud, inviting stares from the other kids. "Sorry, sorry," I said.

My high kept going when I got home. I ran down to my basement, where my room was, and spun around and around in my chair while blasting The Clash.

Rebecca walked in as I was banging my head to "London Calling."

"Kylie?" she said. "Kylie!"

"Yeah?" I yelled over the music.

"Are you OK?"

"Yeah, I just, ah, I love this song!" I said, banging my head some more.

She laughed and looked at me with a knowing smile.

"Oh, OK…I'll be watching TV if you need anything," she said, going back upstairs.

I hid the pills in my underwear drawer where I hoped no one would find them. However, a few days later, after coming home from a trip to New York City with Emma and her step-mom, I reached into my drawer and didn't find them. I turned around, and Mommy was standing in the doorway.

"Don't take those pills," she said. "They're bad for you."

And that was it. She turned and walked away. We never spoke about it after that. And even though they made feel good—something I rarely felt anymore—I never took them again.

Instead, I just had to live with my feelings of depression and isolation.

Even though I had all these friends around me during school, when I went home, I was isolated. Everyone lived on the other side of town, and none of us could drive yet.

Mommy worked sixteen-hour shifts on Saturdays, which meant I'd spend all day alone. I was living with her full-time by this point; I didn't like going to Daddy's because he didn't have a computer with internet. My sisters were usually busy with their own lives.

It was like when I was younger, except now, I was watching depressing movies and smoking cigarettes, a new habit

I picked up behind the local McDonald's with Emma after school. I thought about the fun my friends must have been having, since they all lived within walking distance of each other.

In the spring of my freshman year, I hit rock bottom.

Spring break was rough. I felt so lonely, since my friends were far away and Mommy was working and couldn't drive me anywhere. I spent every night of the week-long break staying up until dawn, watching sad movies and listening to songs about suicide. I couldn't cheer myself up—not even with food, my old go-to.

By the time I got back to school, I was utterly exhausted, with bags under my eyes and new scratches on my wrist.

Right after first period, I went to the school cop.

"I want to kill myself," I told him.

I didn't exactly want to say this, but Lindsay had been egging me on to tell him that.

"I'm so depressed," I'd said to her in first period. "I cry all the time. My life sucks. I don't know what to do."

"You must be suicidal," she said. "I think you need to admit it."

"But I..."

"No, seriously, Kylie. You are going to kill yourself. Let's tell someone. I don't want to lose you."

Lindsay took me by the hand and led me down the hallway.

"You're going to tell Mr. Williamson that you hate your life and you're going to kill yourself," she said. "It's the only way you can get help."

"OK," I said, wiping my tears.

When we got into his office, I told Mr. Williamson what Lindsay instructed me to say. He called my mom to have her come pick me up early.

When she arrived, I got into her car. She was visibly upset.

"What are you doing?" she asked me.

"I'm depressed," I said.

"Well, they told me you can't go back to school without a note from the ER saying you're OK. So let's go."

She took me straight to the hospital, where we sat in the waiting room for nine hours waiting to be seen. I watched *Judge Judy* on the small TV screen and anxiously bit my nails. I hated being in the hospital. The last time I was there, it was when Grandma Jane died. It reminded me of her.

I stared at the TV screen. I felt so awful. *Stupid, stupid Kylie* was going through my head. Why did I do this?

Finally, at 10:00 p.m., the doctor saw me. She had me sit on the hospital bed and asked me a few questions.

"Are you depressed?" she said.

"Yes," I replied.

"Are you taking any drugs?"

"No."

"Are you suicidal?"

I didn't answer. I looked at Mommy, who was sitting behind the doctor, staring at me with her eyes open wide.

"Are you suicidal?" the doctor asked again.

"No," I finally said.

I was in and out in ten minutes. The doctor wrote me a prescription for Prozac and a note that I could go back to school. She recommended to Mommy that I go to a therapist.

"I just paid a thousand dollars for that," Mommy said to me on the quiet and tense car ride home.

"Sorry," I said. I closed my eyes and held my head in my hands. I had a throbbing headache. I wanted to erase the entire day, go back in time, and stop it before it could happen.

The next day, I was at school with my note in my hand. I pretended like everything was normal. I avoided Lindsay after that. I felt like she had manipulated me into doing something I shouldn't have. She'd given me drugs, and that got me into trouble, too. She was a bad influence.

A few weeks later, Mommy sent me to a therapist, a man in his forties in a desolate and far away part of town called Dundalk. His office was dark and cold. There was wood paneling on the walls, and it smelled funny. I only went a few times because I didn't feel comfortable opening up to him. Mommy, who was anti-drug, never filled the prescription for Prozac.

The only other time I tried to hurt myself was about a month later, when I attempted to overdose on Ibuprofen.

I took it from the medicine cabinet and swallowed the pills one by one, in the dark of my room. I felt like I'd never make it out of my house. I'd be stuck there forever. I just wanted to turn my brain off, to have a long sleep, to be done with this depression.

After I emptied the bottle, I immediately told Mommy. I wanted her attention. I wanted real help.

"I just swallowed eleven pills," I said, walking into her room. She was reading in bed.

"Why would you do that?" she said.

"Because I'm depressed," I said.

"Well, don't take any more, or else you'll have to get your stomach pumped. I can't pay another thousand-dollar hospital bill."

I walked out of the room and read until I finally fell asleep.

A few days later, Grandma Riggle came over and brought up my depression. Mommy must have told her what happened.

I was sitting on my computer after school when Grandma Riggle entered the room.

"Hi, Kylie," she said.

"Hi," I said.

She looked at my computer. I had a black and white picture of the singer Ben Folds on my desktop. In it, he was looking down at the ground.

"Who is that man?" she said.

"A musician. Ben Folds."

"Uh-huh. He doesn't look very happy."

I didn't say anything. I just stared at the screen.

"He looks depressed. Why don't you change it to something happy?"

"OK," I said.

"Yeah, that will be better," she said. "God bless you. I'm praying for you."

And with that, she left the room.

I immediately felt angry. Nobody in my family seemed to understand me, and nobody seemed to care. I didn't need Grandma Riggle's false prayers—I needed real help. I needed to be seen. The one person I could rely on, Grandma Jane, was gone. If she were here, she would understand.

I concentrated on my grades and hanging out with my friends while I could. And when I felt down, I wrote about it in my online journal. It was where I could say what I was thinking and feeling and show who I really was so that people could understand me. I longed for it. Every time I wrote in my online journal, I felt a little bit better.

CHAPTER 7

By the first semester of tenth grade, my hormones must have balanced out because I wasn't feeling depressed anymore. Without this constant sadness in the background, I could focus on my schoolwork and my social life.

During this time, I became involved in my school newspaper, writing columns about my life like I did in elementary and middle school. I called it "Trials and Tribulations," and I told funny little stories about my life and ranted about wacky things people did, like pressing the crosswalk or elevator button over and over, thinking it would change anything, or speeding in crowded parking lots. I loved being published every week and having an outlet for my creativity.

I also made more Jewish friends—Nicky and Anath. They were punk rockers like me, except they were much more daring. They drank beer with the homeless punk rock kids in town—many of whom were rich kids rebelling against their parents—and wore dark makeup. They were also loud and opinionated and so confident. I was shy and introverted and afraid of everything. I wanted to be more like them.

Anath and I in particular were close. She was French and Israeli, and she'd invite me for sleepovers at her place. In the morning, she'd serve me instant coffee with sugar and Nutella on toast. She also gave me my first bagels and lox.

"You like this?" I asked, trying it. It tasted strange to me.

"Love it," she said, taking a big bite out of her bagel. "I'm a Jew. This is my food."

Like my other friends, Anath and Nicky lived in Owings Mills, in a Jewish area, which was far from my house. But in the fall of tenth grade, Mommy moved us to Mount Washington, a much nicer part of Baltimore that was closer to everyone. I went from being forty-five minutes away from my friends to about fifteen minutes away.

Mount Washington was also a five-minute drive from Pikesville, where Orthodox Jews lived. I didn't know any Orthodox Jews personally, but I'd see them walking on Saturdays, wearing all black, with the mothers and fathers leading their many young kids. I always wondered: *Where are they walking to? Aren't they hot in all that clothing?*

Pikesville had a Jewish deli, Miller's, which I'd go to all the time. I wouldn't see any Orthodox Jews in there, though. I would see them at the local supermarket with lots of kids in tow. I was baffled by how they handled having that many kids. It seemed so stressful.

I never thought about my future—where I'd go to college, if I'd get married, or if I wanted kids. I'd babysat and thought it was OK, but I didn't have a burning desire to start a family one day. All I was focused on was doing well in school and having fun on the weekends with my friends.

One time, when Nicky's parents were out of town, she had a party at her house, inviting kids from our school.

There, I met a Jewish boy named Ben. He had black hair and glasses and freckles. He wore clothes you'd find at Hot Topic—pants with lots of pockets, a flannel blazer, and band pins on his fedora.

I immediately liked him. We ended up on Nicky's outdoor trampoline, talking about our views on life.

"What do you think this is all about?" I asked him.

"What *what* is all about?" he said, inching his hand closer to mine.

"Life. The universe. What's the meaning of it all?"

"I don't know. Maybe just to have a good time while we're here. What do you think?"

"I think that sounds right. And to be a good person. I don't believe in God, you know."

"Me neither. It seems stupid to believe in God when there's all this bad stuff going on in the world."

"That's exactly what I think!"

We held hands and talked until six in the morning.

That Monday at school, Ben asked me to have lunch with him. A few days later, his friend passed me a note in the hallway between third and fourth period. "Will you go out with me? Check yes, no, or never!"

I checked "yes" and drew a smiley face, giving the note back to his friend and feeling giddy during history class. Ben and I were officially a couple.

We'd hang out in the woods near his home and make funny short films. We'd listen to Patti Smith and the Pixies and talk about the genius of Kurt Vonnegut. We had so much in common. We loved going to punk concerts, where we'd go into the mosh pit together and dance around and laugh.

Ben and his family gave me my first introduction to Jewish rituals. They invited me for Passover, a holiday I'd only learned about on the *Rugrats* Passover special. I didn't know what to expect.

One night in April, I sat with Ben and his brother, parents, aunts, uncles, and cousins around the table as they read from a book and talked about how the Jewish people were slaves in Egypt. During each section, they would have a different custom, like dipping their fingers in their red wine and putting dots on their plates to signify blood or throwing little stuffed frogs on the table.

During the meal, which we finally got to after an hour or so, I noticed a jar of balls on the table floating around in some gelatinous substance.

"What's that?" I whispered to Ben.

"Gefilte fish," he said.

"Huh?"

"Here," he said, putting one of the balls on my plate. "Try some."

I cautiously put it in my mouth. It tasted bland and slimy. I immediately washed it down with the only drink I had, Manischewitz wine. It was sickly sweet.

"Yuck," I said.

"Yeah, it's pretty gross," Ben said. "I can't believe you actually ate it."

We both laughed and held hands under the table.

The longer Ben and I dated, the more comfortable I felt being my true self around him. I told him secrets I'd never told anyone before. I talked about my childhood and how lonely I'd been and how I never thought I was lovable.

"You're so lovable," he said to me one time after I cried to him. "You're so beautiful and cool. You're the best."

"Thank you," I said. "I never felt like this before. I love you."

"I love you, too," he said, hugging me tight.

Over the summer, I got my license, so I was able to see Ben more often. I took a photography class in Dundalk, that faraway part of town where I once went to therapy for a few weeks. I'd finish class at 9:00 p.m. and drive an hour to Ben's house, just to spend an hour or two with him until he went to bed.

Having a car was my ticket to freedom, to not having to be lonely anymore. Even if Ben was busy, I could hop in my car and go sit in a diner and smoke cigarettes and write. I could drive to Anath's and swim with her in her pool or meet Daddy at the movies. We'd go out to The Charles, an arthouse movie theater, and see the latest indie films together.

Mommy was still working constantly and barely around. She was an RN at the nursing home a few days a week and doing real estate on the side. If I didn't have my car, I would have been stuck inside my house all day.

After the summer, when I went back to school, I was in my senior year.

Things felt different the first day of school. It no longer felt like the magical place it did freshman year. Instead, it was starting to feel like prison.

I just wanted to go to college already. I had no idea where I was going—I never thought about it—but I wasn't interested in being in high school anymore. I had a lot of free time at night since my classes weren't demanding. I was bored.

At the same time, Ben was busier than ever; he had taken on a few Advanced Placement classes, and he was in the school play and studying for the SATs. He knew he wanted to get into a prestigious writing program in a college in New York City, like NYU. He was a lot more ambitious than I was, probably because his parents were academics. When he asked me what I envisioned for my future, I didn't have an answer.

"Seriously?" he said. "I've been thinking about college for years."

"Yeah, I just don't care that much," I said.

"Wow, I can't imagine."

Ben and I didn't have as much in common as I thought. We started spending less and less time together, but I didn't mind. He was friends with the theater kids, and they annoyed me. They always tried to one-up each other, and I felt inferior around them.

One Tuesday night, Ben finally had time to hang out at his house. We were watching TV with his mother when I reached for his hand. He retracted it and put it on his lap.

"Are you OK?" I asked him.

"Maybe Ben just doesn't want that right now," his mom said to me.

Ben looked at me sheepishly, but didn't say anything. Later, when he walked me out the door, he gave me a brief hug and said goodnight.

I felt embarrassed. Did Ben's mom know something I didn't? Did he tell her he didn't like me anymore? I was upset that Ben let her do that to me. It felt like a betrayal.

The next night, I went to see Ben in his play. Even though I was upset with him, I still wanted to be supportive. He was great in it; he was funny and made me and everyone else in the audience laugh. I was proud of him.

Afterward, when I went to wish him congratulations and kiss him, he turned at the last minute. I ended up kissing his cheek.

"What was that?" I said.

"We need to talk," he said.

"OK, when?"

"Tomorrow after school. Meet me in the parking lot. I'll see you then," he said, turning back to his theater friends and walking away.

I wasn't sure what had happened, but I had to be honest with myself. My love for Ben had faded. I still loved him, but I wasn't in love with him. It was kind of like what I was going through with my school. I cherished the time I was there, especially at the beginning. Now, I was over it.

The next day, I told him how I felt.

"I think we should break up," I said.

"Me too," he said quickly.

"Really?"

"Yeah. I think it's for the best."

"That's good because I didn't want to hurt you. I really did love you."

"I loved you too."

"What happened?"

"I'm not sure. I think we just fell out of love."

"I think so too."

"I guess we should say goodbye."

"OK. Goodbye," I said, giving him a hug.

I didn't cry because I knew we were doing the right thing. The situation hurt, but there was nothing we could do about it.

I looked back on our time together. He understood me and wanted me, even though he saw my flaws and knew my secrets. He taught me that I deserved love. I hoped that one day, I'd meet a boy like him again, and that when I did, it would last forever.

CHAPTER 8

Senior year felt like a waiting game. I was bored with most of my classes and didn't care much about my grades. I was still working on the school newspaper, which was one of the only things I enjoyed anymore.

I decided that when I went to college the following year, I was going to major in communications or journalism. I wanted to be a writer, but I didn't like creative writing. I always gravitated toward reading newspapers and magazines and nonfiction books. I thought I'd like to keep writing for the newspaper in college and pursue it as a career.

Both colleges I applied to were in Philadelphia, a place I remembered fondly when Mommy would take Rebecca and me to South Street when we were kids. It was there that we'd visit the colorful shops full of kitschy gifts and eat delicious Philly cheesesteaks.

I decided on La Salle, ironically a Catholic school, because they gave me scholarship money. They also weren't heavy on the religious stuff—it felt like a liberal arts college that happened to be Catholic.

Mommy had the idea to purchase a house near La Salle that I'd live in throughout the four years I was there. In that time, the house would hopefully go up in value, and I wouldn't have to live in the dorms.

Nobody from my high school was going to La Salle. Anath and a few of my other friends were still in the eleventh grade. By the time graduation came, I wasn't friends with many people. I was mostly a loner once again.

The day of my graduation, Mommy, Rebecca, Christina, and Grandma Riggle came to cheer me on. Grandma Riggle was especially proud of me. She had emphasized education, and it didn't hurt that I was going to a Catholic school.

"I always knew you were smart," she told me, admiring my cap and gown. "You're going places, Kylie. God is watching over you."

I didn't agree with what she said about God, but I appreciated her kind words.

"You go get your college education and get a good job," she said.

"I will, Grandma," I said.

She gave me a big hug.

"I love ya."

"I love you, too."

Grandma Riggle had softened a bit since I was a kid—or perhaps I saw her in a new light. Now that she didn't pressure me to be religious like she was, I felt closer to her. Hearing "I love you" from her—from a family member—was what I needed at a time when I had no idea where my life was headed.

Those words would live in my head as I transitioned to college life, which would prove to be more difficult than I imagined.

In August, right before school started, I moved into my new home, a row house in a Polish neighborhood of Philly. There were lots of little pizza shops and corner delis. It was full of older people—nobody my age lived there.

Since Mommy wanted to save money on the mortgage, she found a roommate for me. She put an ad on Craigslist and chose the best person who responded. The day after Mommy, Christina, and Rebecca moved me into the house, Arthur, my new roommate, and his father showed up.

Arthur was a chubby twenty-two-year-old Chinese guy with thick-rimmed glasses and acne all over his face. He went to a prestigious university nearby. When he came with his father to the house for the first time, he was very quiet.

Mommy stood next to me and shook Arthur's father's hand.

"Nice to meet you," she said.

"Nice to meet you," he said in a thick accent. "This is Arthur. Arthur, say hello."

"Hi," Arthur said, staring at the floor.

"Hi," I said back.

"OK, well, I'll move Arthur in now," his father said.

Arthur and his father walked up the stairs with just a few bags and a mattress they put on the floor of Arthur's room. Then, his dad left. And so did Mommy. Arthur shut the door to his room, and I shut mine.

I wasn't sure what to make of Arthur. I was too introverted to knock on his door and make conversation. I also felt like he'd reject me if I did that. Living with an older guy just felt awkward, too. I was only seventeen. I resolved that I'd keep to myself and try to focus on school.

Over the next few weeks, I barely saw Arthur; he would hang out at school mostly. When he was home, he'd get takeout. He never used the kitchen. He would get a pizza, eat it throughout the week, then do the same thing all over again the next week.

He also started getting packages delivered to the house. They were huge. I looked at the writing on one of them. "Twinkies," it said. He was getting Twinkies delivered via UPS.

At school, I was enjoying my classes, like Communications 101 and public speaking. But I wasn't making friends that I felt connected to.

Philadelphia, the city I once loved, had changed so much since I was a kid. South Street was now filled with tattoo parlors and drugged up homeless people walking around like zombies. I never wanted to go down there.

I knew that if I had friends, I'd probably end up liking Philly. But since I was so lonely, all the problems around me were magnified.

When I didn't want to go to campus on Friday nights, I'd drive home to Mommy's house in Baltimore instead. It was just too depressing to be alone in Philly all weekend. All I'd do was order pizza and watch my *Arrested Development* DVDs. What else could I do by myself? Going out to eat alone or to the movies or museums by myself didn't seem appealing.

I didn't tell my mom I didn't like La Salle because I felt bad that I wanted to leave the house. I couldn't leave. I'd have to stay there for four years so she'd make some money. I felt obligated to her because she was paying for my college education. Other kids had to take out loans, but I didn't. How could I let her down?

When Sunday nights rolled around and I had to make that dreaded drive back to Philly, I'd inevitably end up crying at some point along the way. I'd be driving alone, listening to some music, looking at the bare trees on both sides of the highway, and thinking about what I was going back to. A school where I didn't fit in. A neighborhood I didn't love. A roommate who wouldn't even talk to me. I couldn't hold back the tears.

I cried a lot during my fall semester. The loneliness was crushing. This wasn't what college was supposed to be like. It was supposed to be the best time of my life, when I could pursue my dreams and party and make lifelong friends. When I could find myself.

Instead, I felt trapped. I knew I had made the wrong decision. I should have worked harder and gotten better grades and higher SAT scores. I was mad at myself for not trying hard enough. If I had, I wouldn't be in this position.

Over winter break, I decided that during my spring semester, I'd change. I'd join the school newspaper and attempt to make friends. I'd spend more time on campus to try to experience what college was really like. I wouldn't give up.

When the spring semester rolled around, I was alone in my house. Arthur was never around; he met a girl at his school and only came home once every few weeks for a night or two. I was grateful for the privacy. I could blare my music and dance around, and the toilet seat was never left up.

I became a weekly columnist for the school paper. I wrote music reviews and little musings about my life, like I did in high school.

I liked the people I was working with at the newspaper. They were students who were older than me and easier to relate to, since we all enjoyed doing journalism. I didn't become that close to anybody, but it helped me feel less alone.

My favorite person on the paper, Joe, was a senior and a great writer. I looked up to him. He would give me feedback and encourage me to keep going.

"You have a real gift," he'd tell me. "Don't give up writing. You should really try to become a full-time writer after you graduate, Kylie."

Hearing this from Joe gave me the confidence to keep going.

Tuesdays were publication days at the paper. Everyone else lived on campus, so they would stay until late at night working on it. I would never stay past 8:00 p.m.; I wouldn't be able to find a parking spot in my neighborhood if I did. It was too dangerous to walk around alone late at night.

But one snowy night, I was having so much fun with everyone at the newspaper that I decided to take a gamble and stay late. When I finally drove home, I was terrified that my 1995 Ford Escort was going to slip off the road and into a pole. I gripped my hands tightly on the wheel and drove slowly, with my hazards on.

When I got to my house, it was midnight. There was no parking out front. I circled around and around my block.

Finally, after thirty minutes, I found a spot several blocks from my house. I parked my car, got out, and immediately fell on the ice and into the cold, wet snow. I felt pain radiating up and down my back and yelped loudly in the silence of the night.

I slowly got myself up, wiped my running nose, and started walking home.

When I got inside, I saw I had a big bruise on my leg.

I had tried to be normal that night. I tried to hang out with my friends at the newspaper and have a good college experience. But I could see that wasn't going to happen.

Instead, I was a loner. I was reliving my childhood all over again. It was suffocating.

I decided I was done with all of it. I couldn't stick it out for three more years. I was just doing it for Mommy, which wasn't healthy. I had to think about myself, about my happiness, about my future.

I was going to leave La Salle.

I started searching how to transfer schools. I decided I'd apply to schools in New York: Fordham, New York University, and the State University of New York at Purchase College. Wherever I got in, I was going to live on campus.

I'd liked the energy of New York when I visited with my family as a kid. I remembered the bright lights of Times Square, being in the back of speeding cabs, and getting delicious deli food from impatient waitresses. It was exciting.

I decided I wanted to pursue journalism as my major. At La Salle, I could only major in communications, but if I transferred, I could major in journalism. I could focus solely on writing and reporting.

I heard about SUNY Purchase through my friend Matty Goldberg, a comedian in New York who had gone there. I'd met Matty a few years prior when he was performing in Baltimore.

Matty was short and Jewish and wore little boys' T-shirts because he was so small. He was also very funny and made self-deprecating jokes about himself.

After I saw his show, we connected online, and I told him about how I was struggling in school.

"You might like where I went," he said.

"Where's that?" I asked.

"SUNY Purchase."

"What is that?"

"It's an arts school near New York City. Everyone there is weird and artsy. You'll fit in."

I set up a tour to see Purchase, and when I got there, I had a good feeling. Like Matty said, I saw lots of artsy-looking people with dyed green hair and mohawks and students carrying around easels and violins and making drum circles. It wasn't the prettiest campus—it was all outdated bricks and run-down classrooms—but somehow, it charmed me. I thought it might be like my high school. The students weren't "normal." They took an alternative path, like I did. They appreciated the arts.

At Purchase, I resolved that I'd finally be among my people again. And so I applied.

❧

After I sent in my applications, I dreaded telling Mommy. What if I didn't get in anywhere? Then I would have told her for nothing. I was afraid she'd freak out, or worse, be disappointed in me.

But it was weighing heavily on me. I felt so guilty. I finally called her and told her.

"Mom, I applied to some other colleges," I blurted out. "I just don't like La Salle. I'm lonely here and—" I started crying "—I don't fit in. I want to go to New York for school. I can't do this anymore."

"OK, if that's how you feel, let's see if you get in anywhere," she said.

"You're not mad?"

"No. If you don't like it, what am I going to do?"

"What will you do with the house if I leave?"

"I'll find some renters."

"Just like that? I didn't know that was an option."

"Oh, sure. It's fine."

After all that, I was so relieved. I wish I had known earlier that it'd be so easy to go.

CHAPTER 9

I got accepted into SUNY Purchase, and that fall, with Daddy's help, I moved into the dorms.

We drove up from Baltimore together, and he carried all my heavy luggage to the new room I was sharing with three other transfer students for the semester.

As he was leaving, he looked around my room. We were the only ones there.

"This isn't too shabby," he said. "Needs some stuff on the walls."

"Yeah, I brought some postcards I can hang up," I said.

"It's good you're majoring in journalism now. I'm sure you'll learn a lot here. Make sure you read *The New York Times.* Then you can really learn how to be a journalist."

"I will."

We stood there silently for a second.

"Well, I gotta get going now. It'll take me a few hours to get back home."

"Thanks for your help, Dad."

"Mhm," he said, giving me a half-hug and walking out the door.

I looked around the room. Though it was bare, I was excited to meet my roommates. I was hopeful about Purchase. I couldn't wait for this new beginning.

❧

Pretty soon, my roommates arrived. There was Megan, a soft-spoken dancer from Massachusetts; Holly, a bubbly psychology major from Long Island; and Quinn, a cool bohemian from New York City who seemed like she was straight out of the '70s.

My journalism classes were much better than the communications ones I'd taken at La Salle. As a journalism major, I felt like I was in exactly the right place. My professor would make us go out and interview students on campus and write a story in two hours. I met people this way and came out of my shell. I had been a shy person all my life, and this was forcing me to talk to people. It wasn't comfortable, but I did it. And I felt proud of myself.

I learned journalism quickly and became one of the top students in the class. I was convinced I was going to become a journalist when I graduated. We were required to subscribe to *The New York Times*, and I tried to read it like Daddy suggested. But a lot of the stories went over my head. I felt like the people in the paper were those New York intellectuals Woody Allen made fun of in his movies. I probably wouldn't become one of them. I was just a blue-collar girl from Baltimore.

During the first few weeks, I partied with my roommates on Friday nights. We'd go to sweaty parties in crammed apartments. I'd drink Miller High Life and dance to loud rap and indie music. On Saturday mornings, we'd get bagels together and reminiscence about the night before.

"Did you see Kylie dance? You got some moves, girl," Holly joked.

"Kylie, you have to teach me," Quinn said.

"Don't ask me. Ask Megan! She's the professional dancer," I said to Megan, who was laughing.

I always hoped my roommates would stick around for the rest of the day, but oftentimes, they wouldn't. Holly would go home to Long Island, Quinn would go to her parents' place in the city, and Megan would hang out with her boyfriend, who'd come down from Massachusetts.

A lot of Purchase students were from New York, and they'd go home on the weekends too. The campus would be nearly barren, and the people who were there were too hungover to do anything.

I didn't want to be alone on campus, so I'd venture into the city. Sometimes, I'd go by myself or hang out with Anath, who was at NYU. There was a lot to do in the city, but if I was alone, I didn't feel comfortable doing anything on my own, just like in Philly. I'd usually just walk around, get lost, frantically call a cab, and go back to Grand Central, where I'd catch the train to Purchase.

I saw Matty Goldberg a few times. We'd eat dinner together and I'd go to his shows. But he was often depressed about his career. One night, he was really down.

"I should just quit," he said as we walked along Bedford Avenue in Williamsburg.

"Matty, you're really funny. I don't think that would be a good idea."

"I bombed so hard tonight. Do you know how hard it is to be a comedian?"

"No."

"You don't get paid. You don't get any respect. There's very little chance you'll make it."

"I don't know what to say."

"I don't either. I think I'm going to stop torturing myself and just quit."

"Well, I don't think that would be a good idea," I said. "I think you should stick it out."

I was young and, despite being lonely and depressed myself, I thought that if you worked hard enough, you would succeed. I thought this was going to be true for Matty...and for myself.

One cold winter night, while trying to help Matty out, I created a Facebook page for him. We hung out in his apartment, and he dictated to me what he wanted his profile to say. After we were finished, I got up to leave.

"I need to go home before the trains stop running," I said.

"I'll walk you out," Matty said.

Just then, the front door opened. A man with brunette-colored hair wearing a black leather coat walked in.

"It's freezing out there!" the man said to Matty.

"Yeah, man. How was your show?" Matty asked him.

"Eh, it was alright."

The man noticed me. I waited for Matty to speak up and introduce us.

"Oh, this is Kylie. Kylie, meet my roommate, Danny Lobell."

"Hi, Danny," I said, shaking his hand.

"Hi, Kylie," he said.

Danny then walked to his room, and Matty walked me out.

I didn't think about Danny again. I also didn't realize how momentous this meeting would be. It'd be two years before fate stepped in and I'd meet him again.

CHAPTER 10

At Purchase, I joined the school paper, *The Brick*, and wrote arts and culture articles. I got free tickets to Broadway shows and concerts I would cover for the paper and enjoyed the meetings with other students.

By my second semester, I'd moved into an apartment-style dorm on campus, which Holly and I shared with two other roommates. We had our own rooms and kitchen. I lucked out and felt like I had the best of both worlds: privacy and the chance to live on campus.

I was doing well academically and with my extracurriculars, so I ended up getting an internship at CBS News in Manhattan. I thought it would be glamorous. Maybe I'd see Katie Couric in the hallway. Perhaps I'd get to interview celebrities. If I stuck it out at CBS, I might even become a famous newscaster there.

My first day on the job, I arrived at the Metro-North station a few minutes before my train arrived. It was rush hour, and there were about a hundred other people waiting for the train. When it stopped, people crammed on board. I couldn't find a seat, which meant I had to stand for the next thirty minutes wearing my heavy backpack.

As soon as we got out at Grand Central, everyone ran to get to work. I looked down at my paper I had printed with directions on it. I found the subway and hopped on, hoping it was the right one. I turned to a man who was wearing a CBS hat.

"Excuse me," I said. "Does this go to CBS on 57th Street?"

"Yes," he said.

"Oh, thank you. I'm an intern there. This is my first day."

"Congratulations," he said. "I'm sure you'll enjoy it."

We chitchatted until we reached our stop. When we got out of the subway, it was pouring down rain. I found a free *amNewYork* newspaper and put it over my head. As soon as I got to a deli, I bought an umbrella.

The umbrella worked for two blocks until a gust of wind came and turned it inside out. Now I had nothing.

For the next four blocks, I walked as fast as I could to get out of the rain. When I made it inside the CBS building, I was soaking wet. I wrung my hair out as much as I could and used some napkins in the bathroom to dry it some more.

"Great," I thought. "This is a bad start."

I found the elevator and made my way up to the eighth floor. Then, I went to a door. Inside the small, windowless room was a carpet that was old and stained. There were three people silently working at computers. They were wearing hoodies and had headphones in their ears. One woman got up when she saw me.

"Hi, I'm Leah," she said. "You must be Kylie."

"Yes, nice to meet you."

"You too."

"Alright, so have you ever logged and transcribed tapes?" she said, showing me an older computer with some tapes and a tape deck next to it.

"No," I said. "What does that mean?"

"Well, you just watch the tape and transcribe what people say in it. You have to time code everything too."

"Ok. I can do that. How many tapes?"

"You can start with five."

I sat down and began the mind-numbing work of logging and transcribing, almost falling asleep several times. This was definitely not what I imagined my internship would be like. There was no Katie Couric here.

I spent the entire semester logging tapes and running errands. Nothing exciting happened but at least having CBS News on my résumé looked impressive.

In my junior year, along with being on the school paper, I joined the school's TV station, where I co-hosted a news show based on the stories we wrote in *The Brick*. I tried to make it funny like *The Daily Show*, one of my favorite shows, because I loved how Jon Stewart communicated the news.

One Tuesday, I went in for the weekly meeting, and there was a guy dressed in a black peacoat, holding a Razor scooter and drinking a Diet Pepsi. He said funny things at the meeting and looked like he was straight out of the '80s, like John

Cusack in *Say Anything*. I learned that his name was Jared, and I was instantly intrigued.

Just a few days later, I found him on Facebook and messaged him.

"Hi," I said. "We both work at PurchaseTV."

"I know. I remember you," he said.

"I thought you were pretty funny in the meeting. How fast can you go on your scooter?"

"Oh, I don't know. But it's my primary mode of transportation. I can do tricks on it. I'll show you sometime. ;)"

Jared was my type: funny, Jewish, slightly out of shape, and quirky. And he obviously liked me. We talked all night on Facebook.

A few nights after we first talked, Jared and I went out to dinner. Our conversation flowed. We had a lot in common. He also had a show on PurchaseTV and wanted to work in media and liked comedy. We both had a rough time with our suburban upbringings. He was the youngest in his family, just like me, and his parents were divorced, too.

"What was that like? It was really tough on me," I said. "I was too young to know it, but it did affect me."

"Yeah, I split my time between my mom and stepdad's on Long Island, and my dad's in the city," he said. "I don't know how my mom and dad ever got together. They're totally different. They didn't get along at all."

Jared and I would spend most nights together, hanging out in his dorm room or mine.

Whenever we were out in public on campus, though, he'd make a point not to make it seem like we were in a relationship. He wouldn't hold my hand at the dining hall or take pictures with me. When a friend snapped a photo of us and tagged him on Facebook, he immediately removed the tag.

"Why did you take the tag off?" I asked him.

"I, uh, just don't want people seeing it," he said. "I'm a private guy."

I didn't think much of it, but this issue kept coming up.

When school was going back into session after spring break, Jared asked me to take a detour to Long Island to pick him up.

"Sure," I said. "Where am I going?"

"You can just pick me up at the grocery store," he said.

"Why not your house?"

"Um, I just don't want my mom knowing how I'm getting back to school."

"Oh, OK," I said.

This bothered me, but I assumed it was just too early for him to introduce me to his mom.

When we got back to school, I showed him the plaid shirts I'd picked up for him at the thrift store in Baltimore over spring break. I'd missed him and thought these shirts were his style.

"Hey, thanks," he said, giving me a kiss.

"You look great," I said, smiling and taking a picture of him with my phone.

"Now, don't post that. That one's just for you," he said, winking.

I didn't know what was up with Jared, but I didn't press him. Instead, I ignored that gut feeling I had that this wasn't right. I liked being with him and I didn't want to do anything to jeopardize it. I could play along if I had to.

❧

On a Wednesday afternoon after journalism class, I received a phone call from an unknown number in New York City. I picked it up.

"Hi, is this Kylie?" the voice on the other line said.

"Yes," I replied.

"This is Jen from *The Daily Show* with Jon Stewart. We'd like you to come in for an interview. How's next Thursday at noon?"

I couldn't believe it.

A few months prior, Matty Goldberg had encouraged me to apply for an internship at *The Daily Show*. He knew how much I loved it; I'd gone to two tapings that past summer and watched it every night. Matty was friends with the executive producer and said he'd be happy to put in a good word for me. I immediately submitted my résumé.

The day of the interview, I walked into *The Daily Show* headquarters in Hell's Kitchen. It was so surreal. I looked around for Jon Stewart, hoping to catch a glimpse of him. The two associate producers of the show, who were both named Jen, met me at the entrance and took me to a nearby meeting room.

Jen Number One and Jen Number Two sat me down.

"You know, we had a thousand applicants," Jen Number One said. "We'll do a hundred interviews. And we'll hire ten people."

"Wow," I said.

"Congrats," said the other Jen. "You're one of the hundred. You should be proud."

"Thank you," I said.

I talked about my experience at CBS and how much I loved *The Daily Show.* They asked me about my career aspirations.

"Well, I'd love to work here one day," I said. "Journalism is so important. And making it entertaining is how you get people to actually pay attention to it."

The Jens smiled and nodded.

"Great answer," Jen Number Two said, making a note of it on my résumé.

When it was over, I got up and shook the Jens' hands.

"We'll let you know soon," Jen Number One said. "Just remember: This is very competitive. *The Daily Show* changes people's minds. We have the power to change the world. So, we don't take who we hire for this internship lightly."

"Yes, of course," I said.

I walked out of the interview not knowing if I was going to get the internship. I checked my email multiple times every hour over the course of the next two weeks, but nothing came in. I was anticipating that I'd soon get that form email that said, "Thank you for applying, but we regret to inform you..." I just couldn't imagine I was as experienced as the other interns. I didn't have much confidence in myself. I started looking for other internships for the next year in the meantime.

Then, one day, I found out I got *The Daily Show.* When the email came in, I jumped up and down in my dorm room. The fall semester of my senior year, I was going to be working every Monday and Tuesday at the show. I kept imagining meeting Jon Stewart, becoming a writer on the show, and having this huge career. I was going to be big.

I told my roommates, I told my friends, I told my parents, I told Matty. Everyone was so happy for me.

Everyone except for Jared. He was scooting by me on campus when I yelled the great news to him.

"Jared, I got *The Daily Show!*" I said.

"Wow, good for you," he said sarcastically, without slowing down. He kept continuing on.

I thought, *What was that about?* I was stunned.

The only thing I could think was that he was jealous of me. He was also into comedy and writing, and I'm guessing he thought he deserved the same opportunity.

However, he never applied to any internships or put much effort into his schoolwork. He smoked a lot of pot and mostly stayed in his dorm room. I didn't see why he should be upset.

I began to analyze the relationship more closely in my head after that. Why didn't Jared want to be seen with me? Was I an embarrassment? Why wasn't he happy I got that internship? Didn't he want me to be successful? Didn't he see how much I cared about him?

I didn't think much about it before because I had low self-esteem. But once I got the internship and people around me saw I had potential, I felt better about myself. I was going somewhere, I thought. And Jared, the one person who should have been my biggest cheerleader, wasn't there for me. I just didn't have the courage to break it off. He was going to have to do it.

And pretty soon, he did. We met up at my dorm room, as usual.

"I think we need to take a pause," he told me, as we sat on my bed.

"I think so, too," I said.

"Look, it's getting toward the end of the school year. You have your internship to prepare for, right?"

"Yeah," I said, looking at the floor.

"So I'll see you around," he said.

"Sure."

I wasn't heartbroken. I had too much to focus on. I was too busy. I was running the school newspaper and doing my show on campus TV and getting more involved by serving on the student council. I had made friends on the council, and they invited me to their parties on Friday nights. I filled up my free time by hanging out with them.

I didn't think about Jared for the next few months. If he would change, would treat me better, maybe I would take him back, I thought. But I couldn't be with someone who was going to drag me down.

At the last party of the year, I was drinking with my friends on the council. I was sad that they were graduating and worried about the next year. What was my senior year going to look like? Was I going to be lonely again? Would I do well at *The Daily Show* and have a career after I graduated? It was 2009, and the world seemed to be upside down, with the recent crash of the housing market and a bad recession. It all felt so overwhelming.

These thoughts were running through my head as I downed beer and tried to drink away my worries. Then, I saw Jared walking by. He spotted me and reversed course.

"Hey," he said to me.

"Hi," I said, taking a swig of my Bud Light.

"Can I talk to you?"

"OK."

We walked over to a hammock on the quad, where we lay and looked up at the trees overhead swaying in the wind. It was early May, and the air was warm and smelled fresh, like flowers.

"I miss you," he said, looking into my eyes.

"Well, you really hurt me," I said.

"I'm sorry."

"You weren't good to me. You should have been happy for me when I got *The Daily Show*. You should have supported me."

"I know."

"It was really messed up."

"I'm sorry. Can we start over?"

I sighed.

"Only if it's going to be different this time. You can't treat me that way again."

"OK. I won't. I swear."

I looked up at the tree.

"Do you love me, Jared?"

Jared held my hand.

"I think I'm starting to."

I smiled at him. This was all I ever wanted out of him: a nice boyfriend I could love who would make me feel special. Who loved me.

I was hopeful—foolishly—that things were going to be different this time.

CHAPTER 11

I spent my summer at Purchase giving tours to prospective students. Jared and I would switch off visiting each other on the weekends; I'd go to Long Island, where I finally met his mom and stepdad, or he'd spend a few days with me on campus. I talked to him about how excited I was to start my internship, be done with school, and get a TV job in the city.

"Yeah, I think you could totally do that," he'd tell me. "Just put your mind to it."

Halfway through June, Jared told me he loved me, and I said it back. This was the first time I'd been in love since high school.

I finally felt secure in my relationship. I thought that this time, Jared was committed to me. And who knew? Maybe we'd last throughout senior year, and then we'd graduate together and get married one day.

Everything was going well, until we got back to school. The second week of my fall semester, right before I was about to start at *The Daily Show,* I got a text from Jared.

"Come over," he said. "We need to talk."

I knew what "we need to talk" meant. I didn't want to go, but I knew I had to. I slowly walked over to his apartment and thought, *Please don't let this be happening.*

When Jared opened the door, he wasn't happy to see me.

"Hi," I said.

"Hi, Kylie," he said, "Come in."

We went to his room, where we sat on his couch. He wouldn't look me in the eyes.

"Yeah, it's, uh, not working out anymore," he said.

"Why? Everything seemed fine," I said, my eyes filling with tears.

"I just don't want to be with you," he said.

"I…we…we didn't even fight," I said, now full-on crying. "Why are you doing this?"

"I just can't be with you."

"Why? Don't you love me? I love you," I said, reaching for him, but he moved away from me.

"I think you should go."

He escorted me out the door. I cried all the way back to my room.

The next night, I got so drunk that I found myself at Jared's door at 2:00 a.m. He came out looking surprised.

"Why did you dump me?" I said, stumbling. "Don't you love me?"

"Shhh," he said, putting his finger to my lips. "Just go home, Kylie. I can't talk about it."

"Fine," I said, once again crying on my walk back home.

When I passed by the other students who were out partying, I covered my face so they wouldn't see me. My eyes were red and itchy, and my black eyeliner was smudged everywhere. I stumbled into bed and fell asleep nauseous, with tears in my eyes.

Every night for three weeks straight, I couldn't sleep. I would cry for hours. I felt alone and abandoned. The warning signs were there, but I ignored them because I wanted so badly to be with Jared. I loved him. He loved me. But I guessed it was all a lie.

And then I started my internship at *The Daily Show,* which made everything worse.

CHAPTER 12

My internship began early in the morning on Monday, and I wouldn't have made it there on time if I slept at school. Anath offered me her couch in her dorm in lower Manhattan so I could get there on time.

My first night in the city was rough. After Anath went to bed, I lay on her couch, tossing and turning, taking out my cell phone every few minutes to check the time. The later it got, the worse my anxiety got. My body felt hot. I kept getting up and going to the bathroom. I thought about how I was going to screw up the next day on the job because I was going to be so exhausted.

Finally, I fell asleep at 3:30. I woke up in the morning to a honking cab outside. I felt groggy. My head was swirling.

I got out of bed and got dressed, then headed over to my internship.

The subway was stuffy and packed. I hardly fit. I had to squeeze in between two people and find a slim spot on the subway pole where I could fit my hand so I wouldn't fall over when the train stopped. I felt a cold sweat dripping down my neck.

When I finally arrived at work forty minutes later, the producers were there to greet me and the other interns. My eyes felt heavy.

I found out that all the interns went to Ivy League schools…except for me. They were wearing suits and nice dresses. I was in an uncomfortable button-down top and my only pair of too-tight dress pants, still sweating from the subway. My face was red.

"OK," said Jen Number One to all of us interns. "Who wants to go on a grocery run?"

The Jens looked around and stopped at me.

"How about you, Kylie?"

"Sure," I said, wanting to be a good sport and also knowing I had no choice.

They handed me a giant list of things to get at the gourmet market six blocks away. I walked out the door, rushing as much as I could.

I had thirty minutes to collect everything: eight different kinds of milk, a variety of fruits, candy for the crew, dried meats, and cheese for snacking on. As soon as I got to the dairy aisle, I couldn't find whole milk, the first thing on the list. What should I do? Was I supposed to call my producers? I didn't want to bother them.

My heart started racing. I just got the milk that was in stock and hoped it wouldn't be a problem.

I realized as soon as the groceries were bagged up that I didn't have a cart to take back to the studio. I picked up the ten bags and strategically placed them on my arms. They were heavy.

By the time I got to the building, my arms had gone numb. There were red marks all over them.

I told the Jens I was back and going to put the groceries away.

"OK, just cut the bagels and put them in the writers' room," Jen Number Two said, waving her hand at me.

I looked at the kitchen counter and saw two dozen bagels. I cut them and placed them nicely on the platter with different types of cream cheese, moving everything around so it would look beautifully presented. I walked over to the writers' room, where there were eight men and women sitting in a circle and discussing that night's script.

I took the tray of bagels, tiptoed into the room, and placed the tray just outside of their circle.

Nobody looked up when I came in or thanked me when I left.

When I got back to the main workspace, I asked the Jens what they needed helped with next.

"Just log and transcribe tapes," Jen Number One said. "That should keep you busy. We'll let you know if we need you again."

I looked up at the clock. It was only 10:00 a.m. For the next seven hours, I went through old news stories and speeches from politicians, typing what they said. By the end of the day, my eyesight was blurry, and I was exhausted.

I thought *The Daily Show* was going to be exciting. That I'd learn about TV production and comedy and maybe even land a writing job myself.

But so far, it was turning out to be just like CBS, another internship where I'd do grunt work, and it seemed like nobody cared about or appreciated me.

Tuesday morning was more of the same. I logged and transcribed tapes for hours, until Jen Number Two came and fetched me from the tape room.

"Hey, Kylie," she said. "We're going to need you to go get some gift bags, OK?"

"Sure," I said, popping out of my seat. "Where?"

"They're in Midtown. I'll give you the directions."

On the cab ride over to the gift bag office, I pictured that I'd be bringing back some goody bags for the guests. Maybe I'd be able to hand them to the guests who were coming on, like Al Gore and comedian Susie Essman.

When the cab pulled up to the building, I went inside.

"I'm here to pick up gift bags for *The Daily Show*," I told the guard, sounding confident. It felt great to be able to say I worked for *The Daily Show*.

"The elevator isn't working," he said. "But they're on the eighteenth floor."

"Oh, well, when will the elevator be up and running again?"

"Who knows?"

My heart skipped a beat. Would I have to walk up eighteen flights of stairs?

I determined that I'd wait it out for twenty minutes and see what was happening. I didn't want to call Jen Number One or Two about it because I didn't want to bother them. At the first meeting with the interns, they told us that when we ran an errand, we should come back as fast as we could so we wouldn't waste any time.

Was I going to get in trouble for this?

I looked at my phone. Five minutes went by. Then ten. Then fifteen.

"Any update, sir?" I asked the guard.

"Nope. Could be out all day."

Now, twenty minutes had passed. I knew what I had to do.

I started the trek up the first flight of stairs. This wasn't so bad. I kept going.

Two, three, four. The floors kept going up and I wasn't out of breath yet.

I'll be OK, I thought.

Five. Six. Seven. It was getting harder to breathe. I had to stop at the seventh, bend down, and catch my breath. I looked at my phone. It had now been thirty minutes. I needed to go faster.

I ran up the next two flights of stairs. When I got to the ninth floor, I felt dizzy. I leaned against the wall. Only halfway there.

I decided to try and see if the ninth floor down was open. When I found it, I pulled the handle. But it was locked.

Crap, I thought.

I couldn't go back down now. It would look bad if I came back to work empty-handed.

When I got to the eleventh floor, I felt a buzzing in my pocket. Jen Number One was calling. I answered.

"Are you coming back soon?" she asked.

"Yeah, the, uh, the elevator broke, so I'm going up the stairs," I said.

"OK, we'll see you soon," she said, hanging up.

I focused on the word "soon." If I was going to get back within a reasonable amount of time, I'd have to hustle.

I took the stairs two at a time and sang an upbeat song to keep going. Twelve. Thirteen. Fourteen.

My heart felt like it was beating out of my chest. I was sweaty and could feel my face was hot red.

Fifteen. Sixteen. Seventeen. Eighteen.

I knocked on the door of the eighteenth floor.

Nobody came.

"Oh, come on," I said.

I knocked louder. And louder.

Finally, a man opened the door.

"Yes?" he said.

"I'm here...to get...the bags...for...*The Daily Show,*" I said, out of breath.

"Did you just take the stairs?"

"Yes. The elevator is out of order."

"Man. That happens all the time. It takes them so long to fix it. Come over here."

He led me to a pile a huge gift bags that must have weighed ten pounds each. They were filled with alcohol, gourmet snacks, flowers, and commemorative merchandise. I picked all five of them up at once.

"Can anyone help me with these?" I asked.

"No, we don't do that," the man said.

I took the gift bags over to the elevator and set them down. I pressed the down button. Nothing happened.

I couldn't believe it.

I sighed and walked to the stairs. By the time I made it down the eighteen flights, my arms were sore. I had to drag the gift bags across the lobby and then outside, where it was pouring rain, and hail a cab.

When I got back to work, Jen Number One was waiting for me.

"Good, you're back," she said. "But why are they wet?"

"It was raining outside. It started pouring," I said.

"OK, well, next time, let's make sure that doesn't happen."

And that was it. I left the gift bags in the hall and went back to logging tapes until the day was over. On the train ride home, my arms and legs felt like they were on fire.

❧

The semester started out with Jared breaking up with me. My internship wasn't going as planned. And then I found out I was failing one of my classes, which had never happened before.

It was a class on the Middle East. I knew nothing about it, but I wanted to take it because the professor had a good reputation.

The first day of class, I learned what it was about: Israel and the Palestinians. I knew the two were in conflict, but that was the extent of my knowledge. Israel just seemed like some religious place in the middle of nowhere.

The professor taught us how, after the Holocaust, the Jews were given land in the Middle East that they established as

Israel. Many of these Jews were highly educated lawyers who used their skills to deceptively take homes and land away from the Palestinians. They then changed the laws on the poor Palestinians so they couldn't get their property back. The Jews were sophisticated colonizers stealing from a native people. It reminded me of the story of Christopher Columbus coming to America, though it sounded much more calculating. I became infuriated at Israel. How could they do that and get away with it?

During one of the classes, a student raised his hand.

"I'm Jewish, and Israel is my people's homeland," he said meekly. "We weren't stealing it. We were going back to where we rightfully belonged after the Nazis slaughtered us. We had nowhere else to go."

"Well, that is just one side of the story you were taught," my professor said. "You have to take the emotion out of it and see there is much more to it."

The student sank in his seat and didn't speak up again. That would be the last time I'd see him in the class.

One Friday night about halfway through the semester, I was drinking with some friends when I ran into a girl from my class. She might have been Jewish.

"Wow, Israelis are real jerks, huh?" I said, tipsily.

"Yeah, they're awful," she said.

"I never knew."

"Me neither."

I thought I was becoming so enlightened through this class. But it turned out that the professor wasn't so impressed with me. I got a D on my first test, and he called me in to meet with him.

"I don't think you understand the course material," he said.

"I believed I did, but I guess I was wrong," I said.

"Maybe you should consider dropping the class."

My face got red. I felt the tears forming in my eyes. I was a good student. I'd never dropped out of a class before.

"I just don't think this class is right for you," he said. "What do you think?"

"I…I guess I'll drop out," I said.

"I think it's for the best."

I felt like a failure.

Back at *The Daily Show*, I did what the producers wanted and asked for more work when I could. I didn't really socialize with any of the other interns or anyone on staff, which I saw other people doing. I was too introverted.

On a Tuesday morning one week, Jon Stewart walked into the kitchen, where I was cutting bagels for the writers.

"How's it going?" he said.

"It's good," I said. "It's so nice to meet you."

"Yeah, you too," he said. "Thanks for working so hard. We really appreciate it."

"Of course. It's my honor."

Jon grabbed a bagel.

"Thanks for this, too," he said, taking a bite. "Delicious."

Jon Stewart had talked to me. This was one of the main reasons I wanted the internship—to get the chance to see him work up close. And that afternoon, I did.

I was assigned to work with the audience coordinator, so I spent the day calling audience members and confirming that they were coming to future shows. Around three o'clock, I went outside to the people waiting in line and took them to their seats inside.

There was a buzz in the air. It was exciting. I was excited for the audience. I knew they were in for a good show.

After the warm-up comic finished his set, the DJ blared "Born to Run" by Bruce Springsteen, and Jon came out and drummed on his desk and said hi to the audience.

"Who's pumped to see the show?" he yelled.

Everyone erupted in applause.

"Who's here to have a good time?"

Even louder applause.

"So let's do this!" he yelled, then ran over to his seat and smiled for the camera.

I thought this internship wasn't so bad. If I could work with the audience like this, I'd love it.

I hoped I'd get to do it again. It would make all the other annoying stuff I had to do much more worthwhile.

❧

It was hard to be back on campus. I was always afraid I was going to run into Jared. My other roommates had boyfriends; I was the only one who was single and alone. I was still the editor at the school paper, but everyone on my staff was younger than me, and I found it hard to relate to them.

I was staying up until five in the morning every night because I couldn't sleep. I was anxious about being alone, about my grades and the class I dropped, about my internship. And, of course, about my future.

Halfway through the semester, all of it caught up with me. I contracted asthmatic bronchitis. I had a rattling cough and was spitting up phlegm and had to use an inhaler to take a deep breath. I also had to call out of my internship twice. I was only there two days a week, so it didn't look good.

I heard the disappointment in Jen Number One's voice the second time in two weeks that I called out. But I couldn't go in. I was coughing every two minutes and couldn't think straight.

"I'm so sorry, I can't come in today," I told her, whispering because it was all I could do.

"OK. See you next week, Kylie," she said, and hung up.

I was worried that being sick would affect my future chances of getting hired at *The Daily Show*. I knew if I could get past the internship stage and become a production assistant, I'd do a great job there. I'd go on to become a writer, and then who knew? Maybe I'd even run the show one day. I was hardworking and determined.

When I recovered from my cough and went back to my internship, it was more of the same: logging and transcribing and running errands. I didn't get to work with the audience coordinator again. I didn't see Jon Stewart again, either.

The other interns would stay late, sometimes until midnight, working on the next day's show. But I couldn't. I couldn't show up too late to Anath's because she would be asleep, and I couldn't stay late on Tuesdays because I wouldn't have a way to get back to campus. The school shuttle stopped running at eleven. I missed out on opportunities that the interns who lived in the city got to do.

I started drinking heavily every weekend to cope with my reality. I would have a few beers, and when I felt that buzz, I'd switch to the harder stuff, like mixed drinks with cheap vodka. I wanted to numb the pain. I wanted to forget.

I'd start off drinking with my roommates and then end up drinking alone, stumbling across the campus and back to my room.

One Saturday night, I drank so much that I felt dizzy as I walked through the quad on a very cold night. It was forty degrees out and I wasn't wearing a jacket. But I wasn't cold. Drinking kept me warm.

The last thing I remember from that night was stumbling into bed at 4:00 a.m. When I woke up a few hours later, I discovered that I'd gone to bed in my clothes. My eyes were stinging, and my body was sore.

And then I looked at the floor. In the middle of the night, I'd thrown up on my senior project, fifty pages I'd worked hard on for the past semester. I held my fingers to my temples and sighed. I had a blaring migraine.

I cried and tried to fall back asleep, but the pain was too much for me to handle. I got up, showered, and went to the dining hall, where I ate a greasy breakfast alone.

I was in a personal hell I'd made for myself. I was suffering and I had no one to turn to. I should have tried harder to make friends. I should have gone for a guy who was going to be nice to me. But I just kept messing up.

I was desperate to turn things around. To get some relief. I wanted to graduate, to get out of there, to get on with my life. Maybe, just then, the curse would be lifted.

❧

Right after I ruined my senior project, I decided to get some help. I signed up to go to therapy at my school once a week.

I met with a fifty-something-year-old woman with short gray hair and colorful glasses. She wore corduroy pants and talked in a low tone, almost a whisper.

As I talked about losing Jared, getting sick, and not feeling like I was doing well at my internship—along with all my other problems—she patiently sat there and listened. I would stop and catch my breath and wipe my tears, which is when she would analyze me.

"It sounds to me like you have anxiety and depression," she said.

"I've been anxious my whole life," I said. "I've been drinking to calm my nerves. And it helps with the sadness, too. I just feel like my life is out of control."

"Well, Kylie, there are ways you can gain back that control. Have you tried deep breathing?"

"No. In fact, I probably forget to breathe sometimes."

"That's normal. Where do you feel your anxiety?"

"In my chest."

"That makes sense. You panic, you stop breathing properly, and you feel a tightness in your chest. Let's take a deep breath."

The therapist showed me exactly what to do, to hold my breath and close my eyes and then let it all out. Push out the anxiety, push out the worry, push out the depression. Let it go.

We sat there in silence with our eyes closed and breathed for a minute. It was calming. My thoughts stopped racing. I was able to be in the moment for once.

"How was that?" she asked.

When I opened my eyes, it felt like I had been asleep.

"It was nice," I said.

"Please make sure you come back every week. We can breathe together. I can show you how to be mindful. Things are going to get better."

Those were the words I needed to hear. And as it turned out, they were also incredibly prophetic.

CHAPTER 13

It was now December. I'd fully recovered from my cough and was going to therapy every week, which was helpful. My anxiety wasn't as bad anymore. And my internship at *The Daily Show* was almost over.

I gave up any hope of getting a job on the show. I could tell the Jens didn't like me. I didn't know how to play the game, how to be social and always have a smile on my face and go along with what they wanted. The last day of my internship really proved that.

As the other interns, producers, and I ate pizza, everyone reminisced about the past semester.

At one point, the producers asked us a strange question.

"So who do you guys have a crush on here?" Jen Number One said.

Jen Number One was married to the executive producer. I felt like messing with her and blurting out, "Oh, your husband! He's just so cute!" and then walking out the door like a boss.

But instead, when the Jens went around the table, asking the question to each of us, I nervously said, "Uhhh, Jon

Stewart." I didn't actually like him, but I liked that he said "hi" to me once in the kitchen. "He's great."

After lunch, each of the interns met with the Jens for a wrap-up interview and evaluation. I'd been dreading it. When they called my name, I walked into their office, my hands shaking.

"Kylie, I know you were only here two days a week, but it seemed like we never saw you," Jen Number Two told me. "For example, our production assistant Caitlin used to only intern here two days a week, just like you, but she did so much during that time. She made herself indispensable. Do you understand?"

"Yes," I said, holding back the tears.

"It just seems like you didn't like it here or something. You never asked for extra work," said Jen Number One.

I was thinking: *Yes, I did.* All the time, I'd go up to them and ask what to do, and they'd just tell me to log and transcribe more tapes.

But I wasn't a fighter. I didn't want to confront them. I knew what was going on. They just didn't like me. And if they didn't like you, you didn't get ahead. So I nodded in agreement to get out of there as fast as possible.

"Yeah, I understand," I said.

"Uh-huh. Well, good luck to you," said Jen Number Two.

I shook both of their hands, walked out of the office, and took off my official Viacom badge, disappointed that I didn't stand up for myself or excel at the internship that I thought I would.

But I was also overjoyed that it was finally over.

A week later, I turned twenty-one. My roommates held a party for me, and I danced to my favorite music all night, making sure not to drink too much.

When the clock struck midnight on my birthday, a Jewish guy named Jacob—who knew I always dated Jewish boys—yelled out, "Alright, Kylie, go on a chair. It's your bat mitzvah!"

Jacob and some other guys hoisted me in the air on a chair and I laughed and laughed.

Maybe things were turning around. I so desperately hoped they would.

CHAPTER 14

Matty Goldberg invited me to his last comedy show in New York before he left for Los Angeles. He was moving to LA to be near his sister, a big-time Hollywood producer. He was going to give comedy a try in a new city. He wanted to get on TV.

I went to a small dive bar in the middle of Greenpoint, Brooklyn, on a dark and chilly night, and watched Matty and a few other comedians perform.

After the show ended, people were gathered in circles around the room. I overheard a man with a beard talking about how he interned at *The Colbert Report.* I excitedly approached him.

"You interned at *Colbert?* I interned at *The Daily Show.* I just finished a few weeks ago, actually," I said.

"Oh yeah?" he said.

"Yeah."

At the same time, we both blurted out, "I hated it."

"No way!" I said. "No one ever said that. Everyone acted like they loved it. They were all Ivy Leaguers. I didn't fit in at all."

"Me neither. I used to have to get Stephen Colbert his sandwich every day, and he'd never even look up to thank me."

"What kind of sandwich?"

"Ham."

"On white bread?"

"Yeah. And no sauce."

"Boooooring!" I said.

We both laughed.

"It feels so good to finally be able to say this," I said. "I held it in all semester. It was literally traumatizing."

"It feels good for me too."

I took a pause and then extended my hand.

"I'm Kylie."

"I'm Danny."

Danny looked familiar, but I didn't know why. At the time, I didn't remember that he was the same man I'd met at Matty's apartment a few years prior.

"So how do you know Matty?"

"I'm his roommate."

"Oh yeah? And what do you do?"

"I'm a stand-up comedian."

The group of people around us slowly started to walk away toward the bar as we stood there talking.

"That's awesome," I said. "Why didn't you perform?"

"Well, Matty had a few farewell shows, so I performed at the other ones. I was off tonight."

Matty walked up behind Danny and put his hand on Danny's shoulder.

"You ready to go, big man?" Matty said.

"Yeah."

Danny turned to me.

"Nice to meet you," he said.

"You too," I said, smiling.

I gave Matty a hug.

"I'll miss ya, kid," he said.

"You too, Matty. Enjoy LA. Let me know when you land. And please soak up the sun for me. I'm freezing."

As Matty and Danny walked out the door, I noticed a funny feeling in my stomach. It was like when I was a kid, and I'd swing really high, and when I came back down my stomach would drop.

I'd never felt that with a guy before. I knew immediately that I wanted to see Danny again.

I didn't know if Danny was single or interested in me. Since I'd been so unlucky with love, I put it out of my mind. I just needed to focus on getting through the rest of the school year and graduating.

But a few days later, fate stepped in, and Matty called me.

"Hey from sunny Los Angeles," he said.

"How are ya? How is it?" I asked.

"Much better than crappy New York. Are you freezing your butt off there?"

"Of course I am. I'm jealous."

"So anyway, what are you up to, kid?"

"Bored out of my mind, as usual. I want the school year to be over already. I'm just waiting it out."

"Hm. Well, why don't you intern for Danny? I know he's always looking for interns."

"Intern for him doing what?"

"He has this comedy radio show. He was the original podcaster. He interviewed George Carlin on his show and always has these interns working for him. Maybe you could greet the guests or something."

"That sounds amazing."

"I'll tell him to give you a call."

Shortly after that, I was walking on campus when my phone rang. I looked at my phone. It was an unknown number.

"Hello?" I said timidly.

"Hi, is this Kylie? This is Danny. Matty's friend."

"Hi," I said. "How are you?"

I stopped walking and put down my backpack so I could give Danny my full attention.

"I'm good. Matty told me you're interested in an internship at my radio show."

"Yes, I am."

"Cool. Well, do you like comedy?"

"Of course. I love it. I saw George Carlin on campus last year."

"Did Matty tell you we had him on our show?"

"Yeah, that's awesome. He's the best."

"We've had on a lot of great people. So, um, are you good at typing?"

"Yep. I can type a hundred words per minute, actually."

"Wow, that's great. Can you take notes?"

"Sure. I can do that."

"Good. So why don't you come to our studio this Friday and give it a try?"

“I’d love to,” I said excitedly.

“OK, I’ll text you the address. See you then.”

“I’m looking forward to it.”

I hung up the phone and smiled from cheek to cheek. I couldn’t wait to see Danny again.

CHAPTER 15

When I arrived at my internship at 9:00 a.m. on Friday, I didn't see Danny at the building, CUNY Baruch, his alma mater where he recorded the show. I waited outside for thirty minutes, anxiously checking my phone and watching the traffic of New York City rush by before hearing back from him. Then he texted, "I'll be there soon, sorry!"

He pulled up a few minutes later in a taxicab and hurried into the building. I followed close behind.

"Chris will be here in five minutes, so can you just bring him upstairs?" he said.

"Chris? Chris who?" I asked.

"Chris Hardwick," he said, rushing up the stairs to get ready.

"Chris Hardwick? Are you serious? I used to watch him on MTV when I was a kid."

"Oh, that's cool. Yeah, so just bring him up as soon as he gets here."

Danny rushed up the stairs to go set up. I waited at the reception desk for ten minutes. Then, Chris Hardwick walked into the building.

I was starstruck. He looked just like I remembered him. He was handsome and well-dressed.

"Hi, Mr. Hardwick," I said to him, shaking his hand. "I'm Kylie. I'm going to take you up to the show."

"Sure thing," he said. "Thanks so much for having me."

I walked up the stairs with Chris. When we reached the top, there were so many different rooms. I had no idea where to go. I didn't see any signs for *Comical Radio.* Danny forgot to tell me where which room the studio was in.

I turned left and said, "Just this way," pretending I knew exactly what I was doing.

We kept walking and walking, but I couldn't find anything. I called Danny, but he wasn't answering.

"Sorry," I said, turning to Chris. "This is my first day."

"That's OK," he said. "No problem."

I took Chris another way and kept searching. It had already been five minutes of this. Suddenly, Danny popped out from behind one of the doors and said, "Hey Chris! Welcome!" and quickly brought him on air.

I was flustered, but the interview ended up going well. Afterward, Danny pulled up a chair next to my desk.

"How was that?" he said. "It's exciting, huh?"

"The interview was really great," I said.

"Sorry about earlier. I know I didn't show you where to go. I was in a rush this morning."

"That's OK."

"I promise it won't happen again."

"I believe you," I said, meaning it. "Don't worry about it."

The following Friday, Danny invited me to come to his Brooklyn apartment, where he worked on the show sometimes. I took the L train and ended up in Bushwick, a quaint neighborhood with old-school townhouses, corner bodegas, and hipsters everywhere.

When I arrived, I rang the doorbell to Danny's apartment. I stood outside waiting for two minutes. Nothing. I knocked. I waited. Nothing.

I called him. He didn't answer. I waited three minutes and then called again.

I stood outside, wondering what to do. Did I get the date wrong?

I knocked on the window next to the front door. Nothing.

I called one more time.

After ten minutes, Danny came rushing out and opened the door.

"Sorry, I was in the kitchen, and my phone is dead!" he said, exasperated, his face red. "Please, come on in."

Normally, I would have been upset. But somehow, I wasn't. Danny was bad at timeliness and organization—that was for sure. But he was also genuinely apologetic. I could tell he felt bad. I could tell he wasn't doing it on purpose.

When we got inside, I felt right at home for some reason. His place was messy and smelled a little moldy, but it was also so homey.

Danny's dog, a cute pit bull puppy, jumped up and licked me. She was one of the most beautiful dogs I'd ever seen.

"Who is this cutie?" I asked.

"That's Juno. She likes you already! That's a good sign," Danny said, winking.

We got to work right away. We sat across from each other at his small kitchen table, typing on our computers, and I noticed he would look up at me over his computer every once in a while and smile.

"How are you doing over there?" he said around lunchtime.

"Good," I said. "Are there any dream guests you want to have on?"

"Hm. I think it'd be great if we could get Jim Davis on."

"Seriously? The *Garfield* guy?" I said, laughing.

"Oh yeah. I love *Garfield*. Don't you?"

"I mean, it's a classic. But have you seen *Garfield Minus Garfield*? That's even better."

"No, what's that?"

I went online and pulled up some comic strips of Jon, Garfield's owner, all alone. Without Garfield in it, Jon seemed bored, depressed, and crazy. Danny and I looked at a few of them and laughed.

"These are funny," Danny said. "What a good find."

"So anyway," I said, turning my computer back toward me, "yes. I will try to get Jim Davis on for you."

"Thank you."

I figured out pretty quickly how to reach out to Jim Davis via his website. I wrote a professional email, and by the end of the day, Jim Davis was confirmed to be on the show. I told Danny.

"You're amazing," he said. "That was so quick."

"Thank you," I said, blushing. "Maybe it's just beginner's luck."

"I doubt it," he said, smiling.

I looked up at the clock. It was 5:00 p.m.

"Well, I guess it's time for me to go," I said, placing my laptop in my backpack.

"Hey, um, do you want to order some pizza?"

"Oh, sure. If you don't have anywhere to be."

"No. Not for a while. Do you?"

"The parties on campus don't start until about ten."

"Then I'll call in for a cheese pizza," he said.

Danny and I sat together on his couch for two hours, eating pizza and talking about college and comedy and what I was going to do after graduation.

"I'm not applying to any jobs yet because I'm still not sure what I want to do," I said. "But I did see an ad for an internship at *The Onion* for the summer. I applied there last year and got rejected, so I don't know if it's worth it to try again."

"Do it! You'll get that internship. I just know it," Danny said.

"Thanks," I said.

"Just do me a favor and keep working at this internship part-time if you can. I don't want to lose you so soon."

I blushed and felt that sensation in my stomach like I did the first time we met.

Danny was such a contrast from Jared, who was jealous of my internship. He was so encouraging. It was refreshing.

"Well, I should get the 8:15 train home," I said.

"See you next week," Danny said, walking me out the door.

I thought about Danny the entire weekend.

He was so different than anyone I'd ever met—and he was so different than me. I was shy, introverted, and unsure of myself. I was afraid of the world. Afraid I would be judged for whatever I said or did. I was trying to tiptoe through life, not cause a stir or make anyone upset.

Danny was outgoing, extroverted, and fearless. He went on the radio and got up on stage every night in front of strangers and made them laugh. He broke the rules. He was recording in his college radio station even though he'd already graduated. He told me he became friends with Jackie Mason after screwing up an interview with him; Danny charmed his way in using his fun personality and then got an interview with George Carlin, his favorite comedian. Unlike me, he didn't overthink things. When he wanted something, he just took action.

Danny and his world were incredibly exciting to me. I was determined to be part of it.

CHAPTER 16

As the school year wrapped up, I became increasingly impatient and wanted to be done with Purchase. I was bored with my classes, with the parties, with everything. It reminded me of being bored as a kid. I couldn't stand it. I knew that once I got into the outside world, I'd excel. Being in college was holding me back.

One uneventful night, as I was eating the cardboard-tasting dining hall pizza alone in my dorm room, an email popped up in my inbox. It was from Brian, the editorial director at *The Onion*. I'd gotten an interview to be an editorial intern that summer.

I jumped up and down and texted Danny: "*The Onion's* giving me an interview!!!!!" Of course, I received an ever-so-timely text message back the next morning: "So cool!"

I went into *Comical Radio* right before my interview, and Danny wished me luck.

"I'm sure they'll love you," he said. "What's not to love?"

Because of Danny's encouragement, I felt confident that I would nail the interview.

During it, Brian asked me about my interest in journalism and comedy and was impressed by my résumé. I talked about how much I loved *The Onion* and my dream to work there. I could tell it went well.

Then, one week later, Brian called me to ask when I could start working. I was so excited. I told him May 25, a week after graduation. I'd be at *The Onion* three days a week for the summer.

I told Danny when I saw him in person the next day.

"I got the internship," I said, excitedly.

"Wow!" he said. "But I'm not surprised. I told you you could do it."

That day on *Comical Radio*, Danny's cohost, Myka, brought me up on air. I thought Myka was devastatingly cool. She was a stand-up comedian who made inappropriate jokes and acted like she didn't care what people thought about her. I really wanted Myka to like me. I was surprised to hear her mention my name.

"So how about our intern, Kylie?" she said.

"What about her?" said Danny.

"Well, she's so quiet. Doesn't that freak you out?"

"No. She's a nice girl."

"I didn't say she wasn't nice. She just doesn't really have a personality. She's kind of a robot."

I felt my stomach sink. Danny paused.

"She's quiet, sure. She's probably just intimidated. She's young."

"Uh-huh."

"Anyway, I won't have anyone saying anything negative about my Kylie. Let's move onto something else."

My Kylie?

I wondered if it was a slipup. As upset as I was about being called a robot, Danny more than made up for it. If he meant to say that, then perhaps he liked me too.

❧

My internship at *The Onion* was starting in just a few weeks, and I had to quickly find a place to live in New York City. I didn't know where I'd go. Would I have to live with some random strangers? Was my rent going to be super expensive?

I told Matty about my dilemma.

"Why don't you go live with Danny?" he said. "I know he's been struggling to pay the rent since I left."

"How much is the rent?"

"It's twelve hundred dollars a month. I slept on the couch and paid six hundred dollars. I bet you could rent it for the same. And you'll be twenty minutes from Manhattan."

"That's a good idea," I said, enthusiastic about the possibility of living with Danny.

I called Danny up the next day and asked him if he was open to the idea.

"Yeah, that would be great," he said. "I need help paying the rent anyway. You could take my room. I'll be a gentleman and take the couch."

I was so happy. I was going places. I was leaving college and working at my dream internship. I was moving in with Danny. My hard work had paid off. I thought, *New York City, get ready.*

A few weeks before graduation, I went into Manhattan to see Danny do stand-up. He was playing at Comix, a club in Hell's Kitchen. When I arrived, he was performing in a small basement for fifty people.

In his act, he did amazing characters like a Scottish grandma and an Israeli uncle reading *Humpty Dumpty.*

"When I was growing up, I had a lot of Israeli relatives, and they would change my bedtime stories on me," he said. "Like, 'Humpty Dumpty, he sat on the Western Wall, he had a very big fall. It was an incident we blame on the Palestinians, all the King's horses and all the King's men, could not put him back together because there was blood and guts and body parts splattered all over the street. Hamas claimed responsibility for the fall. Two hours later, the IDF surrounded the compound in Ramallah. Fifty people killed, sixty people injured, a night of terror and bloodshed. Sweet dreams, Danny boy!'"

The crowd erupted in laughter.

Danny also did over-the-top facial expressions and clever jokes with punch lines I didn't see coming. I'd been to comedy shows before, but seeing Danny was like going to one for the first time all over again. When he got off stage, I was gushing.

"You were so good," I said.

"Thanks."

"No, seriously. You're like, the best comedian I've ever seen."

"Well, I'm flattered."

After his show, we went to another club, Stand Up NY, and got drinks. We sat at the bar, and I revealed my insecurities about graduating.

"I'm scared I'm not going to do well at *The Onion,* just like I sucked at *The Daily Show,*" I said, sipping a Blue Moon.

"You'll be great," he said. "We were doomed to fail at Viacom. They were jerks. We aren't jerks."

"I guess that's true."

"I have some really exciting news for you."

"Oh yeah? What's that?"

"The apartment is almost ready. I just have to give the roaches an eviction notice. Tell them to be out by Wednesday."

"That's disgusting," I said, laughing.

"I'm only kidding. I took care of it a while ago. You should have seen our place before. We used to have flying cockroaches. I couldn't get rid of them. Matty said they were his friends."

"Now that's hilarious."

"One time, I hired these two big Russian guys to come and exterminate my apartment. All they did was turn the lights off, then turn them back on again and stomp around my kitchen killing the cockroaches while screaming at them in Russian. It didn't work. Of course."

"I hope they didn't charge you!"

"This is New York. It was a hundred bucks!"

We both laughed.

We talked for hours until I realized it was 11:00 p.m. The shuttles back to my school from the train station would have stopped running at that point, so Danny suggested I come over and sleep in his apartment.

"Sure," I said, feeling a bit nervous. Was he expecting something from me? After my last breakup, I wasn't ready for that.

When we got to his place, Danny turned on *Hannah and Her Sisters,* one of the Woody Allen movies I hadn't seen.

We sat far from each other on his couch. Right when we got to the dramatic scene where Michael Caine declares, "I have my answer!" Danny's front door swung open, and in barged a guy with tattoos all over his body and long, wet hair. He was wearing a red bandana around his wrist and carrying two plates.

"Danny!" he yelled. "I made fish sandwiches!"

"All right!" said Danny, taking one of the plates.

The man turned his eyes toward me.

"Ay yo, who's this?"

"That's Kylie," Danny said. "She's my intern at *Comical.* She's gonna be moving in here next week."

"Yeah, son!" the man yelled, slapping Danny's hand. His voice suddenly turned formal and he stuck out his hand. "I'm Blanco. Nice to meet you, Kylie."

"Kylie, Blanco is my neighbor."

"Yeah, Danny is my homie," Blanco said.

Suddenly, three huge pit bulls stormed through the front door and ran over to Juno to play.

"That's my crew," said Blanco. "Mama, Daddy, and Lilly. That's Juno's family. She was born right next door in my crib."

"I got Juno from Blanco when she was just a puppy," Danny said.

"Yup. Don't you forget it. She know where she come from. Not from you white people. She gangsta. Ah-ha!"

Danny laughed.

"Anyway, I'll let you two get back to your fun. Whatchu watchin' anyway?"

"Woody Allen."

"Maaaan, that's some white people crap. Get outta here. Ah-ha! Mama, Daddy, Lilly, motivate!" Blanco yelled at his dogs, who stampeded out the front door. The door slammed shut, and it was quiet again.

"Wow," I said, turning to Danny. "He's a character."

"Yeah, he's a good guy. We got our chicken and rooster together."

"You have a chicken and rooster?"

"I never showed you? You'll hear them in the morning. Except the rooster is kind of defective. You never know when he'll go off. He was raised in a dark slaughterhouse before we rescued him, so his internal clock is out."

"You're so interesting," I said. "Who gets a chicken and a rooster?"

Danny took a bite out of his fish sandwich. "You want some?"

"Sure," I said.

Together, we watched the rest of the movie, eating the sandwich but never getting closer to one another. When it came to an end, Danny said goodnight and slept on the couch, while I went into his room. His bed was cozy and smelled nice.

I felt like I was already home. When I was growing up, I never felt comfortable at home. When my parents were together, things were unstable because they weren't happy, and then Mommy moved us every few years. I didn't like where I lived at La Salle, and the dorms at Purchase also felt transient. But Danny's place felt lived-in, like he had fun there, like there was love all around.

I slept so well that the next morning, I had to run frantically out the door to my graduation rehearsal.

"Do you want to stay for some coffee?" Danny said as I was rushing to get ready.

"No, I can't," I said. "I have graduation rehearsal, and I'm super late."

I heard the sound of a chicken clucking and looked at the windowsill.

"Oh, my gosh, it's your chicken and rooster!"

"Oh, yeah. That's Juanito and Donya."

Just then, they squawked and jumped out of the way as Juno came barreling in through the window. She jumped up on my leg and I bent down so she could lick my face. Though she was a fifty-pound pit bull, she acted like a puppy, placing her paws on my shoulder and pushing me to the ground so she could slobber all over me. I laughed so much I couldn't breathe. Danny was laughing too.

"Juno! I have to go, girl," I said.

"She loves you," he said.

I pet Juno on the head and said goodbye.

"Go get 'em," Danny said.

I left with a smile on my face and made it back to Purchase just in time for rehearsal.

CHAPTER 17

A week later, I graduated and moved into Danny's apartment.

Mommy and I drove up from Baltimore with my belongings. All I had was some DVDs and bed sheets.

We walked in the front door, and Danny came out and greeted us with a warm welcome.

"Welcome, Miss Wakefield! Hi, Kylie!" he said.

"Hi, Danny," I said.

"Hi," Mommy said. "So where are we going?"

"Just this way," Danny said.

We walked into Danny's apartment and Juno let out a loud bark. Mommy jumped and started backing out. Danny quickly took Juno by the scruff and put her on the windowsill, and she jumped off and into the backyard. Danny slammed the window behind her, and I heard Juanito and Donya squawking.

"Don't worry about Juno," Danny said, laughing nervously. "She's a sweetheart."

"Uh-huh," Mommy said. "I don't like dogs. And did I hear some chickens?"

"That's Juanito and Donya. Juanito is a rooster," I said.

"Oh..." Mommy's voice trailed off.

We all stood in silence as she looked around the place. I could only imagine what she was thinking.

She lived in a nice apartment in Roland Park, the fancy part of Baltimore. Here, there were stains on the walls. The kitchen floor was made of dirty, peeling laminate. The living room smelled vaguely of mold.

"It's charming, right?" Danny asked Mommy.

"It could...use some work," she said.

"Yeah, of course. It's an old New York apartment."

We all stood in silence again. I looked down at the floor.

"Where's the bathroom?" Mommy asked.

"It's over here," Danny said, opening the bathroom door, which was in the kitchen.

Mommy walked into the bathroom, and after a minute, she flushed the toilet and came out.

"Um, where's the sink?" she said.

"There isn't one," Danny said. "I just use the kitchen sink." He pointed to the sink, which was filled with dirty dishes.

Mommy rolled up her sleeves, used the dish soap, and washed her hands. Then, she turned to me.

"OK, I think I oughta get going now," she said.

"Are you sure you don't want to stay for some tea or coffee?" Danny asked.

"No, thanks. It's getting late. Be well, Kylie," she said, half hugging me. "Good luck."

"Thanks," I said.

She scurried out the door. I heard the front door of the building slam behind her as she pulled away.

"Your mom is nice," Danny said. "I think she really likes it here."

"Sure," I said. "It's definitely her dream home."

We both paused—and then burst into laughter.

"Seriously though, I tried my best," Danny said. "I made the couch up for myself and swept the floors. I know it's not perfect, but I wanted to make it as nice as I could for you. What do you think?"

I looked at Danny and at his apartment, and, despite being messy, smelly, and old, he was right. It did have charm. I appreciated how he put so much effort into making me feel welcome.

"I love it," I said. "It looks great."

"Great," said Danny. "Now, finish unpacking your stuff. I have a show tonight."

Danny was producing a live stand-up show for *Comical Radio.* I helped him carry his heavy microphone and amp to the East Village, where the venue was located.

During the show, I noticed a woman in the audience. She was curvy and she had bouncing brunette curly hair. She laughed loudly at every single one of Danny's jokes.

Who was this woman? And why did I get a feeling she was going after Danny?

After Danny got off stage, he sat down next to the woman. I was sitting close by and could hear what they were saying.

"Thanks for coming," he said to her.

"Oh, of course!" she said, excitedly, giving him a big hug. "You were fantastic."

"I appreciate it. How are you doing?"

"I'm fine, just got off work and looking to have some fun downtown," she said, twisting her hair around her finger.

Danny smiled at her.

"Really?" he said with curiosity.

I got up and walked away to the bar. I was confused. I thought Danny liked me. Had I read it wrong? Maybe I was just a friend. After all, it would be crazy to let someone you like be your roommate.

I felt so stupid. My face was flushing as I watched the two of them talk. The woman touched his arm and giggled. She was wearing a low-cut top and red heels.

I never really knew how to flirt with guys, how to make myself appealing. I was always too shy. I got along fine with men, but usually I just ended up being friends with them. If they liked me, I wouldn't have known it.

The negative thoughts kept going through my head. Who was I to think I could just barge into Danny's life and call myself his girlfriend? I was crazy. This whole thing was crazy…moving in with a guy I'd only known for a few months and hoping he liked me. Did I make a huge mistake?

Then, the woman got up. She and Danny hugged, and she walked out, giving me some side-eye as she left.

Danny packed up his equipment and we got up and walked toward the subway. I was quiet.

"Phew, I'm so glad that's over," he said. "I always get so nervous before shows."

"Uh-huh," I said. "It was great."

"Do you want to watch a movie tonight?"

"Yeah, sure."

"OK. Everything OK?"

"Yeah. It's fine," I said, pausing. "How do you know that woman?"

Danny laughed.

"The Jewish world. I met her when I went to Israel for the year."

Great. Another strike against me. She was Jewish and I wasn't. I'd gone through this with a Jewish boy before.

While I used to proudly call myself a *shiksa,* or a non-Jewish woman who dated Jewish men, all that changed when I was in college.

Before Jared, for a few months I dated Lucas, a Jewish boy whose family was not at all religious. But when the topic of my background came up, Lucas mentioned something offensive his sister had said about me.

"Melissa told me that shiksas are just for practice," Lucas said with a grin.

I felt a pit in my stomach. Like I was worthless. Like Lucas was just using me because I was some dumb blonde girl and he wasn't taking me seriously at all.

I couldn't help it if I wasn't Jewish. It was apparently an issue for Lucas' family—and now, was this going to be an issue for Danny, too?

When Danny and I got home that night from the comedy show, we sat down on the couch.

"Want to watch a movie?" Danny said.

"Sure," I said quietly.

He turned on a bootleg DVD of the *Alice in Wonderland* remake he borrowed from Blanco. It was one of those DVDs you purchase on the subway that was recorded with an old video camera in an actual movie theater.

We cracked open some beers and sat next to each other on the couch with only a small pillow between us. We mocked how terrible and strange the movie was and laughed in all the wrong places that weren't meant to be funny. I could sense some tension between us, but it wasn't the bad kind.

About halfway through the movie, I felt Danny's hand reaching for mine. I moved my hand closer to his. Then, by the time the Red Queen and Alice were having their final showdown, we were holding hands.

Danny squeezed mine. I squeezed back.

I turned over and looked at him. He looked at me and smiled.

The movie ended. It was 2:00 a.m. Blanco must have heard the sound turn off because he busted in through our kitchen window and saw us holding hands.

"Oh, yea, Danny!" he said with a big grin on his face, slapping Danny's other hand. "I told you she like you!"

I blushed.

"OK, OK. I'll leave you two alone," Blanco said, quickly shutting the window. I could hear him laughing in the backyard.

"Does he come in every night?" I asked.

"Yeah. Sometimes I come home and catch him mopping my floor. He yells at me for not being clean enough."

"That's hilarious."

"Yeah."

I looked down at our hands.

"So, are you happy you moved in?" Danny said.

"Yes. I really am."

"Me too."

The screen went dark, and the credits rolled, but we didn't exactly notice.

CHAPTER 18

Danny asked me to be his girlfriend a few days later, and I said yes. We then went out for iced coffee at a café down the block, with Juno lying at our feet.

"I really like you, Kylie," he said.

"I really like you, too, Danny," I said. "But I should probably find another place to live, right? I mean, I hope we work out, but what if we don't? It'll be so awkward."

"No, don't think about that. Just stay. It'll be fine."

"Whatever you say," I said, sipping my coffee.

The week flew by, and soon, it was Memorial Day, and Danny was telling me to join him on Long Island to spend the holiday with his family.

"Are you sure?" I asked him. "It's not too soon?"

"Well, I didn't warn my parents that I was dating you, so they might be surprised. But I want them to meet you."

"OK," I said.

I was nervous but happy. For once, a guy wasn't messing with me. Danny was straightforward. He didn't play any games. I wasn't used to being treated so nicely.

When we got to his parents' home, we sat down on a swinging bench with his grandparents. His grandmother was wearing a flowery summer hat, and his grandfather had bifocals and thinning gray hair.

"Grandma, Grandpa, this is Kylie," Danny said.

"Nice to meet you, Kylie," his grandma said.

She patted the bench next to her.

"Here, have a seat," she said.

"It's nice to meet you, Kylie," his grandpa said.

"It's a hot day, huh?" his grandma said.

"Yes, it really is," I said.

"Well, I'm ready for some burgers, Elaine," his grandpa said.

"Here, I'll get you some," Danny said.

He walked over to the grill.

While he was gone, a handsome teenage boy with blonde hair and a pretty girl with curly hair approached me.

"Hello, I'm Yoni," the boy said.

"I'm Jordana," the girl said.

"I'm Danny's brother. It's nice to meet you," Yoni said.

"And I'm Yoni's girlfriend slash lifetime Lobell family friend," said Jordana.

"It's so nice to meet you guys," I said.

They both gave me hugs. I learned that Danny's other younger brothers, Josh and Sammy, weren't around that day.

Everything was going great. I guess I didn't have anything to be scared of.

When Danny came back a few minutes later, I asked him where his parents were.

"I don't know," he said. "Let me go check."

He left me swinging on the bench with his grandparents, who were eating burgers and potato salad. He came back a few minutes later and took me by the hand, leading me inside his house to his mom.

"Hi Eema, this is Kylie," he said.

His mom, a short, stylishly dressed fifty-something blonde woman with black glasses gave me a quick hello and then went back to making the salads. His dad, who had glasses and was dressed in a button-down shirt, did the same, except he was at the grill. I figured they were busy and didn't have time to talk with me, so I hung out with Yoni and Jordana instead.

On the train ride home, I asked Danny about his parents.

"Do you think they like me?" I said.

"Yeah, I mean, what's not to like?" he said. "But I know they aren't thrilled that you aren't Jewish."

"What? Why?"

"Because it's important to them that I date Jewish girls."

"That's absurd. Why does it matter?"

"Look, you don't understand because you're not Jewish," he said, looking out the train window. "My mom's mom is a Holocaust survivor. She lost her family. My parents spent thousands of dollars sending me to a Jewish school. They're probably disappointed that I would bring home a non-Jewish girl after all that."

"So why did you do it?"

"Because I like you. I don't want to upset my parents, but I also want to be with you."

"But didn't you date non-Jewish girls in the past? Didn't you bring them home?" I asked, referring to Katy, a fellow stand-up comic he dated for two years, and Cari, with whom he had a brief relationship before I came along.

"Yeah," he said.

"So what's the difference?"

"They didn't like it then either. Look, don't worry about it. They'll warm up to you."

"It doesn't sound like they will. I can't change the fact that I'm not Jewish."

We sat in silence. I didn't know what to say. Danny kept looking out the window, sitting far away from me.

I felt like I did when Lucas' sister called me a shiksa. She didn't know me, she didn't see me for who I was. She didn't care to get to know me. I was just some fling her brother would enjoy for a while before he got serious.

And now, I felt like I wasn't being seen again. Would people forever judge me because I wasn't Jewish? Was I just practice?

It didn't feel that way to me. I was a good person. I adored Danny, and I was going to treat him right. I was probably going to fall in love with him. I could tell already.

I met this incredible guy, and already it seemed like it wasn't going to work out. Just my luck.

I looked out the train window. A summer flash storm had started. Rain was pouring down the windows. I put my head against the cold glass and watched the lightning.

"Hey," Danny said softly. "Come here."

He came closer and put his arm around me. I rested my head on his chest, closing my eyes and wishing the day had never happened.

CHAPTER 19

Danny seemed to ignore this problem that was threatening the future of our relationship. I wasn't Jewish. How could it work out?

But I didn't care. I thought that everything would work out in the end. Love would conquer all.

So I ignored it too.

We began spending all our time together, aside from when I was at *The Onion* or he was working on *Comical Radio.* I was interning three days a week at *The Onion's* SoHo office, which was big and beautiful.

We had Whiskey Friday happy hours, and I didn't have to do so many boring tasks like I had at *The Daily Show.* I'd have to run an errand every once in a while, but I liked the people I was working with much better. They were nicer, less snooty, and fun to be around. The managing editor and one of the founders, Joe, was a whimsical, friendly guy who would ride around the office on roller skates.

At night, I'd go to Danny's comedy shows in the West Village, particularly at a place called The Village Lantern. I would help him get people into his shows. We'd stay up until the early hours of the morning because typically, he wouldn't get onstage until 3:00 a.m. There would be me and two drunk people in the audience by that time of night. I would laugh loudly at all his jokes.

After the shows, we'd sit on the wooden benches on the subway platform, holding hands and waiting for the train.

At night, the trains came much less often. If we missed it, it could be twenty minutes until another one came, but we couldn't afford to take a cab home. Danny would often run to the subway if he saw it was about to leave and jam himself in the doorway until it beeped and opened up so I could hop in.

We'd have the same conversation on the way home, night after night.

"I wish I was bigger already," Danny would say. "I've worked so hard in comedy for so many years. I want my break already."

"It'll come," I'd assure him. "I believe in you."

"Really? You think so?"

"Yes. I think you're hilarious. I think you're better than ninety-nine percent of the other comedians out there."

I'd put my head on his shoulder, and we'd hold hands and sit patiently until the train finally screeched into the station.

When Danny didn't have shows, we'd go to the laundromat late at night, doing our laundry and sitting in massage chairs and drinking cans of Coca-Cola from the vending machine.

While I was mostly having fun, I was also anxious and feeling the weight of the city on me. I had Danny, but that was pretty much it. I saw Anath sometimes, but I couldn't call her to hang out every day. I didn't have any other friends in New York. I'd lost touch with my roommates from college by that point.

At the same time, I was quickly going broke. *The Onion* internship didn't pay, and I had used my graduation money from Grandma Riggle and two months' worth of rent from Mommy. I didn't use my mom's credit card or have any credit of my own. I had no savings, and I couldn't get a job until my internship was over.

Once, I was walking around the Greenpoint subway stop, looking for somewhere to eat because we had nothing at home. I checked my bank account. I had six dollars. I'd never had such little money. I didn't know what I was going to do.

When I got home, I lay down on the bed and cried into my pillow. Juno came up next to me, sniffed my tears, and licked my face.

"What's wrong?" Danny asked me.

"I'm so broke," I said. "I only have six dollars to my name."

"Oh, don't worry," he said, sitting on the bed beside me, rubbing my back. "I've been broke for years. My bank account is usually in the negative. We'll be fine. We have each other. Let's go to CTown. I'll show you some tricks."

We walked over to the discount grocery store, CTown, where they sold days-old, gray chicken for half the price. We picked some up, along with a loaf of bread, a box of spaghetti, and cheap tomato sauce. It all came out to less than ten dollars, and Danny paid for it with the money he was making here and there from his comedy shows. He made us a delicious dinner when we got home.

Another time, we stayed up all night and went to the local diner at 6:00 a.m. Danny showed me another one of his tricks.

"Here," he said when we sat down. "Watch this."

He ordered us two waters with extra lemons.

When they came, Danny leaned into me and whispered.

"Now, you squeeze the lemon into the water," he said, doing just that, "and then you take the sugar packets on the table and put a few in. Take your straw, mix it up, and here. You try it."

I took one sip and coughed.

"Don't like it?" he said.

"No, not really. It just tastes like gross lemon water."

"Ah. OK. Hold on," he said, dumping four more sugar packets into the water and mixing them in. He slid the glass my way once again.

"Now, how is this?" he said, lifting his eyebrows.

I took a sip.

"Eh, not bad," I said.

"And that, my dear Kylie, is how you make free lemonade!"

I laughed. We ordered an omelet and shared it, making sure to sneak a few sugar packets out so we could make our own lemonade at home.

Another time, it was a sweltering ninety-five degrees outside. I wanted ice cream but didn't have any money for it. We were in Union Square when Danny spotted an ice cream shop.

"Come with me," he said, taking my hand.

We walked into the air-conditioned shop.

"Ah, this is nice," I said. "I wish I could get something."

"Don't worry," he said, going up to the counter. "Excuse me, sir!" Danny said to the pimple-faced teenage boy working there.

"Uh, yeah?" the teen asked.

"Please, can I sample the cookies and cream?" Danny asked, knowing it was my favorite flavor.

"Uh, yeah," he said, handing Danny a tiny spoon with the ice cream on it.

"And one for my girlfriend too, please," he said, turning back and winking at me.

The boy scooped the ice cream into another tiny spoon and Danny handed it to me.

"Thank you," I said, giggling. "That was nice of you."

"That's nothing," he said.

"Sir," he said, turning back to the boy, "can we please try two chocolate scoops?"

"Yeah, whatever," the kid said, handing us the samples.

Danny did this six more times.

"Alright, alright, now we have to make our decision," he said to me. "Which one would you like, dear?"

"The cookies and cream, please," I said.

"One cookies and cream in a cone, please!" Danny said, taking out three dollars in quarters and handing it to the teenager.

The teenager gave us our scoop and we walked out of the shop, licking the ice cream.

"Now that is how you get ice cream," Danny said. "I was so happy I had some money in my pockets."

"That was very sweet of you," I said. "I would never do that. I'd be so embarrassed."

"You do what you gotta do to survive here. I've been doing that for years."

"You need ice cream to survive?"

"I mean..." Danny said, laughing.

We sat on a bench in Union Square and watched old men play chess as we finished our cookies and cream. Danny gave me the last bite.

For once in my life, I didn't feel lonely. I had someone who understood me. I could be myself around Danny. I didn't have to worry about what he was thinking or hold anything back.

Often, I'd wake up in the morning, and Danny would say, "Good morning, beautiful."

"What? No. I just woke up," I'd say, never able to take a compliment.

"You look beautiful," he said. "Come give me a kiss."

"But I didn't brush my teeth yet," I'd protest, holding my hand over my mouth.

"That's fine. Come here."

He was sweet, and he appreciated me. Even though we were struggling financially, I just knew that with Danny's genius, we'd figure everything out.

CHAPTER 20

By mid-summer, I desperately needed money to pay rent. I applied to a bunch of part-time jobs I could work on the weekends, but nobody got back to me. The economy still hadn't recovered since the 2008 meltdown, and I was feeling the consequences.

So, instead of relying on jobs, Danny and I found other ways to make money.

In our neighborhood—which was slowly filling up with trust-fund kids straight out of college—we found a lot of nice stuff left on the curb. We'd walk around and collect sewing machines, coffee tables, and antique chairs, and then we'd sell them on Craigslist, sometimes making a few hundred bucks for ten minutes of work.

We also rented out our living room to strangers on Craigslist. We had a one-bedroom railroad apartment, so we had to go through the public hallway to access our kitchen and bathroom. It was a pain, but it kept us going.

Danny took jobs handing out flyers on the street, going door-to-door for political campaigns, and doing security at nightclubs. He'd sometimes get ten or twenty dollars for doing a comedy show, or, if he was really lucky, a few hundred bucks minus travel expenses.

I started freelancing for the local paper, the *Greenpoint Gazette,* making fifty dollars an article. It wasn't much, but it helped. Plus, I enjoyed freelancing. I wished I could live off that alone.

Danny and I were exploring the city together in the cheapest ways possible. We wouldn't go to Broadway shows or eat at fancy restaurants. We'd grab a sandwich from the bodega, swipe our MetroCards, and take a ride to wherever was nearby.

On a sunny Saturday, we jumped on the Q train and were planning to take it all the way to Coney Island. We were talking about religion, and Danny said he believed John Lennon's philosophy that organized religion was not good.

"The only thing that would matter to me is that I would need to marry a Jewish girl," Danny said casually.

I felt my chest go cold and tears form in my eyes. *Here we go again,* I thought.

Danny saw I was upset, and I could tell he immediately regretted saying anything.

"Look, I don't even want to get married," he said.

He knew this wasn't the right thing to say either. I slid away from him and hugged the sticky subway pole. Danny apologized again.

"Kylie, I'm not breaking up with you or anything. I just want to take it slow. If we ever get serious, we'll discuss it then."

"OK," I said. I didn't know where this was coming from. I never fantasized about my wedding as a little girl. I didn't think about having kids. I still felt like a kid. I never brought up marriage. Why did he?

"Come here," he said.

I slid back over to him, and he held me in his arms all the way to Coney Island. I couldn't stop hearing those words: *I would need to marry a Jewish girl.* Was this relationship going to be over as fast as it had begun? Was he going to kick me out of his apartment? Was I going to have to go home to Baltimore, the last place I wanted to be?

I couldn't go back to that. I had tasted a little bit of the life I wanted, and I knew I'd never be the same. I knew the good life was just getting started. What came before was oftentimes painful, lonely, and depressing. I was determined not to let this go. I was going to build something better for myself. I wasn't going to give Danny up so easily. I was going to fight for him.

I thought, I'll wait this out. If we do decide to get married one day, Danny might change his mind. Love could conquer all. Right?

CHAPTER 21

A few weeks later, as Danny and I were in our apartment, talking, he looked me in the eyes.

"I love you," he said.

"I love you, too," I said quickly.

He smiled and brushed my hair away from my face.

"I mean, is it too soon?" I said.

"Probably. But it's fine."

"We rushed everything else, so why not this?"

"Exactly."

We hugged each other. Saying "I love you" to Danny didn't feel like a big deal to me. I thought it was implied from the moment I met him. It felt like he was always in my life and always would be. While we were different, we worked well together. It was just so natural.

The only thing was, I didn't want to get hurt. I couldn't do it again. It was in the back of my mind. Were things going to turn out like they had with Jared? Was Danny going to suddenly leave me one day?

I mean, could it really be this good?

❧

On a Friday afternoon, when Danny and I were broke, and didn't know where our next meal was going to come from, he said we should go to a place called Chabad for Friday night dinner.

"What's Chabad?" I asked.

"It's a Jewish organization at the rabbi's house. They make free food for Jews. I'll just tell them you're a Jew."

"OK, let's go," I said, excited at the prospect of a home-cooked meal.

When we arrived that evening to the walk-up building on Bedford Avenue, the Orthodox rabbi, Rabbi Shmuly, a thin man in a black hat with a dark, scraggly beard and kind eyes, greeted Daniel with a Jewish joke and introduced himself to me.

"It's nice to meet you, Kylie," he said, nodding his head and smiling. "Good Shabbos."

"It's nice to meet you too," I said.

Danny and I sat at the dinner table, which was full of other non-religious Jews, like an eccentric artist wearing orange-rimmed glasses and a free-spirited 20-something girl with wildly curly locks and a flowing flower dress. They were nice and welcoming to me. The rabbi said some prayers in Hebrew. I tried a piece of bread.

"This is delicious. What is it?" I whispered to Danny.

"It's challah," he said.

I ate four pieces of this doughy, sweet bread.

While the rabbi spoke during the main course, I didn't know what he was saying, even when he was speaking in English. He was saying something about the Torah, which I had never learned about.

I looked around at all the faces in the room. I felt a warmth inside of me that started in my chest and washed over my entire body. I didn't know if it was the challah, the speech, or the sense of community, but I felt euphoric.

This was so different from how I'd grown up, where dinners were silent if we ate together at all.

Shabbat dinner was lively. People laughed loudly. The rabbi was nice to me, a stranger, even though he probably knew I wasn't a Jew. I was opening up to people. The conversation was so natural. I was always more comfortable around Jewish people; this affirmed it.

I asked Danny if this dinner was happening again soon on the cab ride home.

"Every week," he said. "Why?"

"I'd love to come back. It was nice."

"Really? OK."

"I can't believe all that is free. It's incredible."

"Yeah, they get donors to make sure Jews have a Friday night dinner. It's very nice."

"How did you meet the rabbi, by the way?"

Danny then told me the story of how he came across Rabbi Shmuly. He hadn't been religious for many years after being kicked out of *yeshiva,* a Jewish school, for not getting good enough grades in his secular studies. He was transferred to another yeshiva that was poorly run and full of kids who were drug addicts and troublemakers.

"It was awful," Danny said. "When I was praying, the other kids would throw spitballs at me and laugh. I knew that in order to survive there, I had to fit in. I stopped praying and caring about my Judaism."

Eventually, Danny landed in public school, and that set him on a more secular path. He became fully non-observant—save for never eating bacon or shellfish, which was not allowed in Judaism. As he progressed in his comedy career, he started performing on Friday nights, Shabbat, which you weren't supposed to do if you were religious.

For ten years, he didn't care about being observant or spiritual, until one Yom Kippur.

"I'd spent the day in synagogue, fasting and asking God for forgiveness," he told me. "As the sun was setting at the beach, I was so inspired that I said a prayer to God. I told Him I'd keep one Shabbat over the course of the next year. I didn't know why. I just felt it in the moment."

A few months later, Danny was walking on Bedford Avenue in Williamsburg. He saw a rabbi approaching him.

"Are you Jewish?" the rabbi asked.

"Yes," Danny said.

"Then come for Shabbat sometime. Friday night. We start at seven."

"Well, I actually promised God that I would keep one Shabbat this year. But not this week. I have a show."

"OK, when you can come, come. We're here every Friday night."

But Danny forgot all about it.

A few months after that, he was walking on Bedford Avenue again when the rabbi approached him.

"I never saw you at Shabbat dinner!" the rabbi said.

"Oh, I'm sorry, Rabbi," Danny said.

"Don't worry, you can still come. See you this Friday."

Danny went and loved the experience. Not only did he get that delicious food, but also, he loved joking around with Rabbi Shmuly, who was incredibly nice, and he felt the magic of Shabbat he enjoyed when he was a kid before getting kicked out of Jewish school.

Danny knew he must have done something right because, a little while later, he met me. He fell for me right away when we met at the bar, he said, but he wasn't sure if I liked him.

"One night, I got drunk and ended up on my doorstep," he told me. "I looked up at the sky and prayed to God that you liked me. I wanted to be with you."

"Wait. I thought you didn't believe in religion," I said.

"Yes. But I still believed in God. I still prayed in my own way."

"Well, you have very powerful prayers. I haven't prayed since I was a kid. I thought it was nonsense."

"No, I think there's something to it," he said, smiling.

Maybe Danny was right, I thought. He was right about so many other things. Could I have been wrong about God?

I thought about it as we held each other's hands. One thing was certain: I couldn't wait to go back to the Chabad.

CHAPTER 22

Just a few weeks later, we went to Chabad again for Friday night dinner. When we got there, the men and women were praying on different sides of a white screen. I sat on the women's side and opened a prayer book to a random page and read the text in English. I noticed there was a lot of praising God and thanking God for life's blessings.

I zoned out and peeked through a hole in the screen to see Danny, who was closing his eyes. He was singing a beautiful tune in Hebrew in unison with the other men.

This was a side of Danny I hadn't seen before. Normally, he was gregarious and loud. He played pranks on people—he'd call up White Castle corporate and pretend to be a character named "Beefy" who wanted more onions on his burgers. One time, he went to Hollywood as his character Sami the Israeli, an ex-Israeli pop star who gave fake tours of the town and crashed open houses by jumping into fancy pools fully clothed.

Here, though, he was quiet and reflective. He was calm. He looked peaceful.

Was Judaism going to bring out a different side of him?

At dinner, after the praying ended, I asked Danny why we had to praise God so much.

"I learned that it teaches you gratitude," he told me. "The more you thank Him for your blessings, the more blessings you realize you have. You need to pray more than He needs your praise. At least, I think that's why."

That made sense. Was I grateful for my life? I had Danny, an apartment in New York, a cute dog, and my dream internship. Sure, I was broke, but I was also young and had a lot of potential. Maybe if I could learn to be a little more thankful, like Judaism taught, I'd be happier with my life. I wouldn't struggle so much.

At the very least, Judaism was shifting my perspective in a positive way. I could tell already just how smart its teachings were, and I was looking forward to learning more.

Danny and I took a break from going to Chabad when he was offered a month-long comedy tour in South Africa. Since I was now alone in the city, I made sure to see my friends as much as possible.

One Saturday, I hung out with my college friend I hadn't seen in a while, Robin, in her neighborhood of Midwood, Brooklyn. Robin was Jewish but unaffiliated. She showed me around, pointing out her favorite shops and taking me to a sushi bar.

When I was walking back to the subway to go home that night, I passed an Orthodox Jewish man wearing a black hat.

He was carrying a pizza box, and his little kids were excitedly following behind him. How nice it would be to have a family pizza night. This was something I never did with my family.

Now that I was making a life for myself, it was my mission to never feel lonely like I had when I was a kid. I wanted a home that felt alive. I wanted a thrilling life, and I wanted to be surrounded by people who loved and appreciated me.

When Danny got home from South Africa, I experienced what that would be like when he took me to his parents' house for Shabbat dinner the first time.

He'd talked to them while he was away, telling them we were in love, it was serious, and I wasn't going anywhere. It was hard for them because I wasn't Jewish, but at the same time, they wanted to be welcoming and supportive.

One Friday, Danny and I went to their home in Long Island just as Shabbat was about to start at sundown. When we walked in, the house smelled like fresh-baked bread and chicken soup.

In the den, Danny's mom was watching a YouTube video of a man speaking angrily in Flemish in front of what looked like a parliament.

"What's that, Eema?" Danny said, as we walked up to his mom, calling her the Hebrew word for "mom."

"This man is an anti-Semite," she said. "He's spewing hate against the Jews. He's the new Hitler. Anyway, Shabbat Shalom."

She kissed Danny on his cheeks and said hi to me.

"How are you doing?" she asked me.

"I'm good," I said. "Thank you for having me."

"It's good to be home for Shabbat," Danny said.

"It's been a while," she said.

"I know, I know. I missed you," he said, giving her another hug.

"I always miss you, poppet."

She then turned back to her soup and pointed toward the living room.

"I made up your room around the corner," she said. "Get settled in before candle lighting."

We walked into our room, which was dark and had two twin beds in it.

"Uh, what's this?" I said.

"Oh," Danny said. "They're probably not comfortable with us sleeping in the same bed, since we're not married."

"Gotcha. Well, that stinks."

"I know. But those are the rules."

He kissed me on the forehead and put down his backpack.

"Danny, why was your mom watching that video?"

"Well, it sounds like the guy is an anti-Semite. You have to be aware of these things, or there could be another Holocaust, God forbid."

I scoffed. "Really? Come on. That would never happen again."

"Yes. It absolutely could."

I thought they were just being paranoid. How could the Holocaust happen again? How could there be anti-Semitism? It didn't seem fathomable.

When the sun went down, Shabbat started. Danny's siblings and his parents' friends started pouring into the dining room for supper. His mom, dad, grandparents, three brothers, and Jordana and her family were there. Danny explained what was going on with the prayers at the meal.

"We sing 'Shalom Aleichem,' which means 'peace be upon you,' to welcome in the Shabbat angels," he whispered to me. "It sets the tone for the week. If you have a calm Shabbat, the idea is you'll have a calm week. It brings good vibes into your home."

I liked the idea of marking the beginning of the new week, which I learned happened on Saturday night after Shabbat was over. The Jewish days started at night, since the Torah said that God created nighttime before He created daytime. Acknowledging and honoring a new week gave more meaning to the idea of time. Instead of going, going, going, you could stop to acknowledge the passing of time and take a nice break. I thought it could be good for me to slow down a bit, since I was always going a million miles per hour, and my head was racing with anxious thoughts all the time.

Following "Shalom Aleichem," Danny's father sang "Eshet Chayil" to Danny's mom. It translated to "A Woman of Valor." I read how wives worked hard for their families and how their husbands and children would praise them. Husbands sang this to their wives every week to let them know how much they appreciated them.

When "Eshet Chayil" was over, Danny's father got up, placed his hands on Danny's head, and blessed him. He then kissed Danny's head and did the same for each of his three younger brothers. After that, he said the prayer for wine, and we all got up and washed our hands and said a blessing to eat challah. We weren't allowed to talk between washing our hands and eating the challah, so everyone was quiet around the table.

And then, once we ate our bread and could talk again, the table exploded in lively conversation, with everyone talking over each other and asking about their week.

Danny's mom served delicious chicken soup, a Friday night tradition, along with salads, followed by potatoes, vegetables, rice, and a large roast chicken.

The meal seemed to go on forever. I ate so much that I thought my stomach was going to pop. Danny's mom brought out three desserts, and I couldn't resist.

She served something called Turkish delight and fruit salad and fresh mint tea. I hadn't tasted food like this before. It all seemed very exotic.

Dinner was over around midnight. Danny and I got up from the table and plopped down onto our separate beds.

"I'm so full," I said, staring up at the ceiling, clutching my stomach.

"Welcome to Judaism," Danny said.

In the arms of my beautiful mommy in Grandma Jane's kitchen.

Snoozing happily on Grandma Jane's lap.

I was a happy little girl in my favorite chair at grandma's house.

Wearing Christmas reindeer antlers and posing with a dancing Santa, the Victorian village, and my dog, Corky.

Graduating high school next to my proud Grandma Riggle.

One of my many trips back home to my beloved Baltimore during my first year of college.

Danny and I young and in love at a hipster winery near our apartment.

My first time at the Western Wall in Jerusalem.

Danny and I standing at the snowy Western Wall right after he proposed to me.

Ringing the bell at the bridal shop after Danny helped me pick out my dress.

Private
Party
in
Progress

July 30, 2015—the best day! Danny and I got married under the chuppah in front of our family and friends and became Mr. and Mrs. Lobell.

Visiting a synagogue from 1492 in amazing Morocco.

Writing inspiring pieces to fulfill my mission to be a light, an Ora, in this world.

Celebrating Hanukkah with Sophia and Ella, our two little beauties.

In our Moroccan-themed sukkah with Sophia and Ella.

Our little Ella Batya's (fake) honey advertisement for Rosh Hashanah.

With all three of our blessings—Sophia, Ella, and Asher—and a statue of Stitch, of course.

CHAPTER 23

I loved Shabbat dinner and the warm feeling I got from it. Though I was technically an atheist, I was moving away from that label and opening myself up to the idea that maybe there was a God.

After all, I had always believed in fate. It was fate how Danny and I met. It was fate how I always dated Jewish boys, and my good friends were Jewish when I was growing up. These kinds of things didn't just happen. It felt like someone from above was writing my story. It felt like everything that had happened to me led me here. All my struggles had culminated in this. They meant something.

I learned at Chabad that, though our prayers weren't always answered, everything was for the best in God's eyes. Maybe God didn't want something to happen for us because it would put us on the wrong path. I thought back on my own life.

If my ex-boyfriend Jared and I had worked out, I probably never would have discovered God and Judaism, since he was so secular. Plus, I wouldn't be with Danny, whom I connected with much more. He was truly my best friend.

If I'd done well at *The Daily Show*, I'd likely have a good job as a writer—but who knows what that would have done to me. I might have become a less sensitive person since I'd have to work in the cutthroat world of TV.

And if my parents didn't get divorced, they wouldn't have been happy together. They deserved to be happy.

Who knew what God planned for me? And at the same time, who was I to think I knew best?

I discovered that with Judaism, you could ask question after question. Nothing was off-limits. Discourse was encouraged. It was part of the tradition.

I learned about why bad things happen to good people, which was a complex question. I learned that human beings have free choice. If we didn't, and if we just did everything God wanted because we were scared of being punished, our relationship with Him wouldn't be authentic. One of the reasons bad things happened was because we took certain actions that made them happen. Also, Judaism included belief in an afterlife, another world, and we don't know what happens then. We don't know God's bigger plan.

I thought about Grandma Jane—she had died so suddenly. Within a few months of being sick, she was gone. And she died at seventy-six, which wasn't very old. *But,* I thought, *maybe God wanted to bring her home sooner. Maybe she deserved to go to heaven and be with Him. Her soul had completed its mission.* This idea gave me a lot of comfort.

Being an atheist was bleak. Sometimes, I couldn't sleep because I'd stay up trying to imagine eternal blackness and nothingness. Our suffering and struggling were for nothing. We lived, it was tough, and then we died.

But Judaism was totally different. I saw that being Jewish was a joyous way to live, and I wanted in on it.

I was curious what it would be like to be Jewish. I decided to start looking into conversion, and the first step was trying to find a good book on it. I went online and bought my first Jewish book on conversion. It said that if I liked Woody Allen and bagels, I might be Jewish.

"I like those things," I thought.

But from what I was learning, there had to be much more to it than that. I wanted to keep exploring Judaism and see where it took me.

While I felt content during Shabbat, at other times, I was a complete mess. I couldn't sleep at night because I was worried about how I was going to pay my rent and cover the other high costs of living in New York City. I already couldn't afford a monthly MetroCard anymore; I used to be able to purchase the ninety-five-dollar one with ease.

Between Danny and me, we'd scrape together enough money to buy groceries, but I was constantly worried. I also didn't know what I wanted to do with my career. I loved being a freelance writer, but I knew that in the long term, I'd need a higher paying job.

Danny did what he could, but we were both broke.

I would often talk to Danny about how worried I was.

"I don't know how we're going to pay rent next month," I told him once.

"It always works out," he said.

"It's just so daunting. Everything here is so expensive. How am I ever going to get ahead?"

"I don't think you should worry about that. Things work out."

"Aren't you scared?"

"Not really."

"How?"

"I'm just not. Where does worrying get you? Nowhere. We're fine."

"I have eleven dollars in my bank account. How much do you have?"

"Maybe fifty."

"And that doesn't scare you?"

"Nope."

"How?"

"I just have faith it'll be OK."

"I can't live like this. It's too much weight on my shoulders. It's just too much."

"You'll be fine, Kylie," he said, putting his hand on mine.

I could feel my face getting hotter.

"Yeah, well, maybe it won't," I said, stepping away from him. I started having trouble breathing.

"Are you OK?"

"Does it look like I'm OK?" I said, pacing around our room.

"Whoa, where is this coming from?"

Danny tried to hug me.

"Get off me," I said, pushing him away.

"Fine."

He walked away and sat down at his desk. "But I think you need help. You should find a therapist. You have serious anxiety."

"A therapist? How could I afford a therapist? Just add one more expense to my life. That'll make things better."

I rushed outside for some fresh air. I could have moved back to Baltimore, where things were cheaper. I wanted to make it in the big city. I didn't know how I would do it.

Maybe Danny was right. Maybe I did need help. It had worked while I was in college.

There had to be a cheap therapist out there.

When I calmed down, I went back inside, sat at my computer, and Googled "low-income therapist." Danny came over and saw what I was doing and massaged my shoulders. Something called "sliding scale therapy" popped up.

"Look Danny," I said. "Here are a few options."

"Good," he said. "I just want the best for you, you know."

"I know. I'm sorry I freaked out."

"It's OK. It's scary being in your early twenties and just trying to find your place in this city. But don't worry. I'm here for you. I love you."

"I love you, too," I said, giving him a hug.

Danny and I continued switching off between going to Chabad and his parents' house for Friday night dinner.

We also started doing the Jewish holidays together. His parents invited us for Rosh Hashanah, the Jewish New Year, and Yom Kippur, the day of repentance, where you ask God for forgiveness for your sins throughout the year.

Danny came from a Sephardic Turkish family and grew up going to a Moroccan synagogue, where we went for the holidays. I didn't know what was going on; the services went on for hours and hours and hours, and everything was in Hebrew. But the tunes were beautiful. For most of it, I closed my eyes and just listened to the singing. I stood when Danny's mom stood, since we were in the women's section together, and read the English in the prayer book, even though I didn't know the deeper meaning behind it.

On Yom Kippur, Danny told me he was going to fast and that I should try it too. I couldn't eat or drink anything for twenty-five hours. I'd never fasted before, and I was worried about it.

I jumped in headfirst. I ate a ton of food right before the twenty-five-hour fast to hold me over. I stuffed myself with chicken and bread and desserts and drank a lot of water.

The fast was going fine until the middle of the afternoon on Yom Kippur day, when I got a huge headache.

"Danny, I feel sick," I told him, lying down on the twin bed next to his.

"That's normal," he said. "This is the point where that happens. Just take a nap, and when you wake up, we'll go back to synagogue and the last bit will be really easy and go by fast and then it's over. Trust me."

"OK," I said.

I fell asleep for an hour and woke up. Danny was already awake and looking at me.

"Hi, beautiful," he said.

"Hi. Is it over yet?"

"Not quite. But here, I'm going to take you somewhere. Get your coat on."

Danny and I walked to the beach. It was a late fall day and cold outside. No one else was around.

When we got to the ocean, we looked up. The sky was stunning, with bright pinks and oranges and fluffy little clouds dotting it.

"Don't you feel that?" Danny said. "Don't you feel God?"

"Yes," I said. "I really do."

We stood in silence. Danny said a Hebrew prayer to himself, and I looked at the beautiful surroundings. I could hear the sound of the ocean waves quietly rolling onto the shore.

When Danny and I went back for the finale of Yom Kippur at his synagogue, it was very dramatic with loud singing and a nice candle lighting called *havdalah* at the end. Danny was right about the fast; I didn't feel hungry at all.

And then, once I saw the food at the break fast, I felt like I was starving. I ate muffins, bagels, cookies, and pieces of cake, and I drank orange juice and coffee and felt stuffed and sick all over again. But I did it. I had fasted for the first time. I survived.

"How do you feel?" Danny asked.

"I can't believe I did it," I said.

"And you're not even Jewish. You didn't even have to. Look at you, Kylie. You're so spiritual," he said.

"I never thought of myself that way, but maybe I am."

After Yom Kippur, I started praying to God again, just like I did when I was a child. I found that it helped me calm down when life seemed too difficult, when I got too worried about money or my future. I had decided that I did, in fact, believe in Him. The experience at the beach was so powerful. The world was too amazing for there not to be a God. It was an absolute miracle. I don't know why I didn't see it before. It was just common sense that God existed.

In December, right before my twenty-second birthday, Danny and I celebrated another Jewish holiday together: Chanukah. We went to Chabad, where we sang songs as we lit the menorah, and I learned that we ate fried food like donuts on the holiday in honor of the oil that miraculously lasted eight days. I knew a little bit about Chanukah from watching *A Rugrats Chanukah* on Nickelodeon, but Rabbi Shumly explained the much deeper meanings of the holiday to us all.

"Chanukah comes during the darkest time of the year, in the winter," he said. "And during it, we light the menorah, which radiantly shines. Even when the Jews were being threatened, when their religion and culture were being taken away from them, they lit the menorah and found the light. It miraculously burned for eight nights. This teaches us that even in our darkest moments, there can be light. It is the Jewish people's mission to be a light unto the nations, to bring God's love into this world."

I thought, after everything the Jews went through—the story of Chanukah, being enslaved in Egypt, the Spanish Inquisition, the Pogroms, and the Holocaust—their light was still shining bright. All the cultures that tried to kill them died out, but the Jews survived. They were obviously a special people.

I thought, what an honor it would be to become a Jew.

When Christmas came around, I didn't celebrate it. I called my family, and Mommy sent me a card. I never enjoyed the holiday after my parents got divorced. We had those Christmas Eve celebrations with Grandma Jane and Grandpa Bill, which was what I loved most about it. But after my parents split up, it just became about the presents. It always felt empty to me.

Chanukah, on the other hand, reminded me of those early Christmas memories with my family. It wasn't about commercialism; it was about being together and feeling inspired. When it came to Judaism, every single ritual had multiple meanings and interpretations. I found all of it to be fascinating, and I was eager to keep learning more.

CHAPTER 24

I was inspired by Judaism's teachings, but I needed help with my anxiety.

I started seeing a therapist, Jill, at a sliding scale nonprofit in Manhattan. I would go to her once a week and talk about how anxious I was about living in the city. Jill was soft-spoken and in her twenties, like me. I felt like I could open up to her.

"Everything is so expensive," I told Jill. "I don't know what I'm going to do with my life. I have no idea. It just feels like a crushing weight that I'll never be able to get off me."

I could feel the tears coming on. I grabbed a tissue and dabbed my eyes.

"Sorry," I said.

"It's OK to cry," Jill said. "Is there anything you're hopeful about?"

"I'm hopeful about my writing career. And things are going well for Danny and me. I'm also really getting into Judaism."

"Can you tell me about it?"

"Well, I was an atheist from when I was twelve, but then Danny took me to a Friday night dinner for Shabbat, and I feel like I'm believing in God again. Ever since I started believing in Him, it's helped me when I've felt down. And I've also been trying to do Shabbat, which is such a peaceful time. It's when I can finally stop thinking so much about my problems and just take a break."

"That's great. It sounds like you're able to connect with something bigger than yourself, which can really help with anxiety."

"Yes, I think so. I've always felt at home with Jews. Growing up, many of my friends were Jewish, and so were the guys I dated. I think it was all for a reason. Maybe I've had a Jewish soul all along. I might make it official now and convert to Judaism."

"This sounds like a really positive step in your life."

"Yeah, it is. I can already see how it's been good for me, especially during a time when I feel so alone. I love that I have a place I can go to on Friday nights where I can connect with other people."

"That's so important. Is Danny on board with this plan?"

"I…I haven't told him yet. I'm not sure how he'll take it."

"Are you worried?"

"A bit, yeah, because he didn't have a good experience with Judaism. I don't want to discredit his feelings or anything, either. I just hope he gets where I'm coming from."

"I think if you talk about your own perspective and how it's helped you so much, he will understand. I'm sure he only wants the best for you, right?"

I thought about it for a moment.

"Right," I said out loud. But in my head, I wasn't certain about it at all.

❧

I thought about my conversation with Jill for the next few weeks. The more I went over it in my head, I figured out what I had to do. So I made a big decision. And I was going to tell Danny about it over breakfast.

We were sitting in our kitchen one Sunday morning when I spoke up in between bites of my pancakes.

"I'm going to convert," I said.

Danny put down his fork and looked at me for a few seconds. I was nervous. Was he going to tell me not to convert? Did he want me to stay this way so he wouldn't have to marry me one day? Was I ruining the fun he was having? And if he broke up with me, would I still want to do this?

Yes, I thought. The past few months made me feel like I finally belonged somewhere. It was so easy to talk to Jewish people. I quickly fell in love not only with Danny, but with his culture and religion too. Me, an avowed atheist. I couldn't believe it. But here I was. I believed in God again.

"Oh yeah?" he finally said.

"Yeah. I believe in God. I feel like I'm Jewish, like I've been Jewish all along and I just didn't know it."

"Well, that's a big move. Don't do it just for me."

"I'm not. You got me interested in it, but I'm not doing it for you. I'm doing it for me."

"Are you sure?"

"Yes."

Danny paused, thinking.

"Well, don't convert Orthodox. It's too hardcore. And you know my past with it. Maybe look into a Conservative conversion."

I didn't know what he meant, but I was willing to learn more.

"Sure," I said. "Are you OK with this?"

"I guess I don't really have a say, right? You're going to do it anyway?"

"Yes."

"You're so strong-willed," he said, laughing.

"Yeah, I guess so," I said, laughing as well.

That night, I did what I always did as a journalist and took to investigating via Google. I typed in "Jewish conversion New York City" and clicked on the first site that came up.

Within a few hours, I had a meeting set up with a rabbi for the following Sunday. Was it really this easy?

CHAPTER 25

Before Danny and I saw the rabbi, I decided to tell Mommy, Daddy, and my sisters that I was planning to convert to Judaism.

I was nervous. Were they going to think I was crazy? None of them were religious.

I called Mommy first.

"I've made a big decision," I told her.

"What?" she said.

"I'm going to convert to Judaism."

There was a pause. I started nervously shaking my leg.

"Well, that makes sense. You were kind of lonely growing up, and it's good that you'll have a community."

I couldn't believe how she got it right away.

"Yeah. It's a really nice community of people. I like what I'm learning, too."

"Now what? Do you have to go to school or something?"

"I'm not sure yet. Danny and I are meeting with a rabbi. I think I'll have to take some classes, but I'm not sure for how long."

"Well, let me know how it goes."

"I will. Thanks, Mommy."

The conversations with my sisters and Daddy went pretty smoothly, too. He thought it was interesting and told me about some independent movies about the Holocaust I should watch.

I was glad when the conversations were over with and that my family didn't think I'd lost my mind.

Just a few days later, Danny and I were sitting and sharing a sandwich at the Lower East Side deli where the rabbi told us to meet him.

"I'm nervous," I said. "What if he rejects me?"

"I heard they're supposed to reject you three times," Danny said. "It could happen, I guess."

"I just want the rabbi to know I'm sincere."

Within a few minutes, a man in his sixties, the rabbi, walked in. He had a short white beard and was wearing a yarmulke.

"Hello. Are you Kylie and Danny?" he said.

"Yes," we replied.

"Nice to meet you. OK, first thing's first," he said, sitting down and turning to Danny. "Do you like farmer's cheese?"

"Farmer's cheese? Uh, yeah, I guess," Danny said.

"You're halfway there! And how about you…?" he said, looking at me. "If you convert, are you sad you'll have to give up Christmas?"

"I never really liked Christmas," I said. "I found it to be depressing after my parents got divorced."

"Hm, that's very interesting," the rabbi said, scratching his chin. He then turned back to Danny. "Do you like tongue?"

"Yeah," Danny said.

"OK, you're all the way there!" he said, laughing. "We've got a Jewish boy over here!" He tucked his shirt into his pants and turned serious. "Look, I've converted a lot of people. Nancy Sinatra, for one. I don't know if she's still Jewish. Anyway, I give private lessons, and they start at one hundred dollars a class. I don't know if you'll need to take classes for months, or years, but that's what it is. Let me know when you want to start. Nice to meet you."

With that, he got up and left. The whole thing lasted less than ten minutes.

I turned to Danny.

"I have fifty-six dollars in my bank account," I said. "I can't do a hundred-dollar class for who knows how long."

"So don't do it," he said. "He doesn't even know if Nancy Sinatra is still Jewish. What does that mean?"

"I don't know. Is this my only option?"

"No, I'm sure there are others. Just keep looking."

I left feeling disheartened, but it wasn't going to stop me. When I got home, I Googled "Conservative synagogue New York." One near Union Square popped up. I emailed the rabbi and told him about how I wanted to convert, and he invited me to services that Shabbat.

Shabbat morning, I took the subway into Manhattan. Danny was out of town at a gig.

The synagogue was small and mostly filled with older people, but I liked the vibe. It was cozy. At *Kiddush,* the communal meal after the services, the rabbi introduced me to a woman and her husband—she had just converted. They seemed happy.

"Come meet me in my office on Tuesday," the rabbi told me. "We'll discuss everything there."

I was excited. It seemed like I found a synagogue and a rabbi all at once.

When I arrived that Tuesday, the rabbi and I sat down in his office.

"Now, explain to me why you want to convert," he said.

"My boyfriend, Danny, took me to a Chabad for Friday night dinner. I loved it. The more I learn about Judaism, the more the world makes sense to me. I didn't believe in God and now I do. I enjoy doing Shabbat and can't wait to keep learning more. And when I was growing up, all my friends were Jewish. It kind of feels like I had a Jewish soul all along."

"I see," he said, tapping his fingers on his desk.

"I'd like to get started with my conversion. Can you help me?"

"Well, typically we don't do a conversion until you're ready to get married. Are you getting married soon?"

"No, I'm still pretty young," I said. "Danny and I just started dating not too long ago."

"Well, I think it's best if you wait until you're ready to get married and then come back," the rabbi said. "In the meantime, there's an Introduction to Judaism class at the 92nd Street Y. It's very good. I advise you to go there."

"Thank you," I said.

I left feeling confused. Was this a rejection? Should I have said, "No, I want to convert now?" I was only twenty-two years old. I couldn't imagine getting married anytime soon. Was I going to have to wait for years and years to become Jewish?

I didn't let this stop me, though. I found out the next Intro to Judaism class was starting in a few weeks, and the 92nd Street Y accepted credit card payments. I enrolled that night.

When I got to the class, the other students were a bunch of Wall Street guys and their extremely good-looking fiancées. One was a Japanese woman with perfectly straight, silky hair and a nice white blouse. Another was a blonde bombshell wearing stilettos and diamonds. I looked down at my pants, corduroys from Target, and my band T-shirt. I thought I must have looked like such a *schlub.* I'd just learned that word in Yiddish, and it seemed to fit me well.

When the rabbi walked in, I saw he was wearing a brightly-colored knit yarmulke with the Phish band logo on it. He was Rabbi Miller, and he explained that he worked at a Modern Orthodox synagogue and he was excited to teach this class.

The blonde woman raised her hand.

"One question before we get started, Rabbi," she said in a thick Russian accent. "If I become Jewish, does that mean I have to give up lobster?"

"Oh, we'll get into all that, don't you worry," he said, smiling.

I laughed to myself and thought, "Yeah, of course you're going to have to give up lobster, lady. It's shellfish!"

Rabbi Miller spent the first class talking about the basics of what it meant to be a Jew: to believe in God, and only one God.

I learned that if I wanted to convert, I'd have to renounce all my former beliefs. This would be easy, since I didn't practice a religion other than Judaism.

Rabbi Miller explained that Jews follow the Torah, and that traditionally, they believed God wrote it and that Moses, a prophet, gave it to the Jewish people. Judaism was the original monotheistic religion, and other religions—Christianity and Islam, for example—came after it. They had some similarities to Judaism, but also changed the Jewish teachings in the Bible and the Quran.

The Ten Commandments came from Judaism, but there were actually 613 commandments in total. The rabbi said that we could view following the commandments and doing the mitzvahs as a way to connect to God, while sinning was a way that we disconnected from God. And on that note, *mitzvah,* while used colloquially to mean "good deed," simply meant "commandment."

After the brief introduction, Rabbi Miller turned to the blonde woman that asked the lobster question at the beginning of class.

"One of the commandments is to not eat shellfish, so unfortunately, lobster is out," he told her.

With a disappointed look, she crossed her arms.

"But you can still have fish!" the rabbi said, laughing and pointing to the Phish logo on his yarmulke.

I giggled. This was going to be an interesting class, all right.

CHAPTER 26

In the class, Rabbi Miller covered the basics of Judaism: the holidays and calendar, history, lifecycle events, and prayer.

While there were formal prayers you'd say every day, such as the *Modeh Ani* (which meant "I give thanks") prayer when you woke up, or the *Shema* ("listen") prayer right before bed, you could also pray to God in free form.

"The purpose of prayer is to get into a habit of building a connection with God," Rabbi Miller told us. "We can ask God for help, we can thank Him, and we can praise Him. You can ask Him for small things, like help getting a good seat on the subway, or for bigger things, like helping you out financially. God wants us to reach out to Him."

I raised my hand.

"But what if you pray and your prayers aren't answered?" I asked. I thought about my parents' divorce and Grandma Jane's death.

"That's a tough one, I'll admit. Here's the thing: Only God sees the big picture. We can see a small snippet of it, and that's it. What looks bad could be good, and what looks good could be bad. Our job is to trust that even if He doesn't answer our prayers, in no way does that mean He's forgotten about us or doesn't care."

Another student, one of the Wall Street guys, raised his hand.

"Yeah, Rabbi, people in my family died in the Holocaust," he said. "I have a hard time believing that was good."

"I'm so sorry to hear that. My understanding is that what God does is for the best—but we don't know what 'the best' means. This is a classic question: Why do bad things happen to good people? I don't know the answer. I only trust. And with this caveat, so I don't sound Pollyannaish or dismissive, it's totally fine to be mad at God or frustrated. It's normal, even. It's part of our relationship with Him. If it was all good, what good would this relationship be? It'd be a shallow one. He wants us to grapple. It's what makes us more connected."

We were all silent as we let the rabbi's words sink in.

For the first time, I felt some comfort about my past and my relationship with God. Judaism was helping to repair it.

It made me even more certain: I wanted to be a Jew.

CHAPTER 27

One day after class, I asked Rabbi Miller if I could speak with him. We stood outside the 92nd Street Y and talked before I caught my subway home.

"Rabbi, my boyfriend said I should look into a Conservative conversion," I said. "But the Conservative rabbi I spoke to said it was too soon for me to enroll in a formal program. I really want to get started. What should I do?"

He thought for a minute.

"Well, why don't you look for a synagogue in your neighborhood that you can walk to? Start going on Shabbat and see how you like it."

"That sounds like a good idea," I said, hopeful once again.

"Just so you're aware, though, if you get a Conservative conversion, the Orthodox will not accept it. So you could have some problems down the line."

"Oh," I said. "I had no idea."

"Look, there are a lot of politics involved in conversion, unfortunately. But if you have any questions, please let me know."

"Of course. Thank you so much, Rabbi."

When I got home that night, I turned to Google once again, typing "synagogue near me" into the search engine. The first result was a synagogue called The Greenpoint Shul.

I checked out the website. The pictures of the synagogue looked beautiful. I learned that it was started in the early 1900s. I clicked on "Clergy" and saw a picture of the rabbi, Maurice Appelbaum. He was young and clean-shaven and looked like a nice person. I called the synagogue the next day.

"Hello, is this The Greenpoint Shul?" I asked when he picked up the phone.

"Yes, I'm Rabbi Appelbaum. How can I help you?" he answered.

"Well, I'm in an Introduction to Judaism class at the 92nd Street Y, and the rabbi said I should find a synagogue close to my apartment. I live nearby."

"We'd love for you to join us. We have services every Saturday at 9:00 a.m."

"I'd love to come. And do you do conversions, by any chance? I'd like to start my conversion process."

"Yes, we have a conversion program. We meet Tuesday nights at 6:00 p.m. But why don't you start by coming for Shabbat? It would be wonderful to meet you."

"Great. I'll see you there this week."

I was excited to meet the rabbi. And I was surprised that the synagogue was in the neighborhood right next to ours and I'd never seen it before. When Danny came home, I told him the news.

"There's a synagogue called The Greenpoint Shul, and the rabbi invited us this Shabbat," I said. "He was so nice. And he said they do conversion classes."

"What kind of synagogue is it?" Danny asked.

"Oh, I don't know. I didn't look."

"As long as it's not Orthodox."

"But Chabad is Orthodox."

"Yeah, but they won't convert you. I don't want you to do an Orthodox conversion. I already told you."

"But my experience might be different from yours. Have you considered that?"

Danny sat down at the kitchen table and sighed.

"It won't be. You need to trust me on this. I grew up around it. Everyone is being nice to you now, but it will change. You'll see."

"I just don't think it will. And maybe if you give it another chance as an adult, you'll like it."

"I don't know. I don't fit into the Orthodox world. They made that clear. They didn't want me. They're judgy. They're very insular. We wouldn't fit in. I didn't."

"I'm not sure what this synagogue is, but the rabbi seemed very welcoming. I think we should try it. Can you at least try it?"

Danny looked out the window.

"Well?" I said, leaning toward him.

"OK, fine," he said. "But just don't drag me back into all that. I'm done with it. Going to Chabad every once in a while is one thing, but you can't do an Orthodox conversion. No way."

"Of course not."

As I would soon find out, I wouldn't be able to stand by my word to Danny.

CHAPTER 28

When we got to synagogue on Saturday, Danny and I had to sit separately, like at Chabad. I could see him through the openings in the separator between the men's and women's sections, which I learned was called the *mechitza*. He sat and stood at the right times. I watched him for cues during the two-hour long service.

The prayers were in Hebrew, and Rabbi Appelbaum stood at the front of the room leading the services. He was tall and wore a brightly colored knitted yarmulke, just like the rabbi at the 92nd Street Y. He must have been in his early thirties.

I didn't know where we were in the prayer services, and I kept flipping the pages at the wrong times. The woman next to me must have realized that I didn't know what to do. She pointed out which page we were on and kept checking in with me. I whispered a thank-you to her, and she smiled at me.

While the rabbi was praying, his little daughter pulled at his prayer shawl and said, "Daddy, Daddy." He lifted her up and held her in his arms.

After the services were over, some congregants brought out dishes with silverware, and we sat and ate hummus, chopped vegetables, and other types of hors d'oeuvres. Everyone introduced themselves and was so nice. They weren't Orthodox like the people I'd seen in Williamsburg, the nearby neighborhood filled with Satmar Hasidic Jews. They were modern and mostly in their thirties and forties. I told them I was converting, and they all seemed interested in my story.

"Why do you want to convert?" one woman named Marcia asked. She was wearing a baseball cap and a short-sleeved, flowery dress.

"Well, I always had Jewish friends and dated Jewish guys, and when Danny took me to Chabad for Friday night dinner, I really connected with it. I feel like my soul is Jewish."

"That's very profound," Marcia said, smiling. "It makes sense. They said every Jewish soul was at Mount Sinai when we received the Torah, and that must include converts too. Since we were both there, hi again."

I giggled. "Nice to see you again."

"We hope to see you back here next week."

"Me too."

I turned to Danny. I was nervous.

"Did you like the services?" I whispered.

"They were fine," he said, not making eye contact with me and instead concentrating on the crackers and hummus on his plate.

I treaded lightly.

"It's good that you liked them," I said.

I was enjoying myself, and I didn't want this to be the last time we'd come to this synagogue. It was different from my class, where I didn't fit in. Here, I felt like I could have a community. I thought, *Is Danny going to torpedo it?* What would I do if he tried?

❧

After my 92nd Street Y class ended, I began taking Rabbi Appelbaum's class. It was every Tuesday night at the synagogue. There were two other couples. One was the intellectual type, a non-Jewish wife and her Jewish husband who were both in academics. The other was in the arts, and the husband was not Jewish but hoping to convert.

There was also a woman who was converting because only her father was Jewish; in Judaism, you were Jewish if your mother was Jewish or you had a valid conversion.

One of the reasons that Judaism went by the mother is because you always know who the mother is, but you don't know who the father might be. But in general, a mother has a deeper impact on a child than the father. After all, she carries the child in her womb and is typically the primary caretaker. It made sense to me.

Since I was a woman, the law of matrilineal descent would factor into my conversion later.

In the class, we learned about the stories in the Torah. I was particularly fascinated by what Rabbi Appelbaum told us about Noah's ark.

"When the flood was over, God showed the world a rainbow, which was a reminder that He would never destroy the world again," he said. "Now, we have a special blessing whenever we see a rainbow."

I asked the rabbi, "Are these stories really true?"

"There is some debate," he said. "Some say they're true, and some say they're allegorical. Either way, we can learn meaningful lessons from them. For instance, it took Noah forty years to build the ark because God was trying to tell him to get other people to repent during that time. Noah wasn't supposed to only save his family and himself. That's why he wasn't as great as Avraham, who tried to save the people of Sodom and Gomorrah from destruction and death. If we see people around us struggling, we are supposed to help lift them up."

I found this teaching fascinating; Judaism was so rich with similar teachings. I always loved learning, and that's what I discovered Judaism was all about.

When I was a kid, I felt I had so many unanswered questions, and I was never told the truth or given enough information. And as a journalist, I loved asking questions and digging deep to find the truth.

With Judaism, things were out in the open. You could speak your mind. Nothing was taboo or off-limits. It was in the culture. I could look at any Shabbat table on any given Friday night, and I'd see people saying what they wanted and asking about the Torah.

The Torah was true; from there, though, there were so many different interpretations of the mitzvahs and the stories and the concepts. It seemed like a constantly evolving religion that adapted to modern challenges.

I also learned that Judaism didn't stress the afterlife. It made sense to me to focus on the here and now rather than where you'd go when you died.

Being Orthodox, the rabbi said, typically meant that at the very least you keep Shabbat, you eat kosher, you live in an Orthodox community, and you send your child to Orthodox schools. Though I didn't know all the rules involved or the wide range of practice within Orthodoxy yet, this way of life seemed reasonable.

Before I ever decided to convert or went to Chabad with Danny, I thought Judaism just meant that you were neurotic, you ate at delis, and you lifted people onto chairs during bar and bat mitzvahs. I quickly learned that it was so much more than that.

I started writing about my conversion for a site called *Jewcy* and got great feedback. People were telling me that I was inspiring. It was so validating.

One Friday morning, while we were sitting at our kitchen table having coffee, Danny surprised me.

"Do you want to do Shabbat here tonight?" he asked.

"Really?" I said. "What changed?"

"I can tell you're really dedicated to your conversion, and I don't want to hold you back. I don't necessarily like where you're going with it, but we could still celebrate Shabbat."

"Thank you. How do we do this?"

"We'll go to Williamsburg and get challah and wine and meat. Then we'll come back and have dinner. It'll be nice."

"I can't wait," I said, putting my hand on top of his.

❧

In the afternoon, we walked the fifteen minutes to Williamsburg. The signs on the light posts were in Yiddish, as was the writing on the large school buses parked on the street. I saw men with big, circular, furry hats walking around. The shops were old-fashioned, like they hadn't been updated in half a century.

I dressed in a knee-length skirt, but it wasn't as long as the skirts the other women on the street were wearing. They were wearing wigs and hats on top of their wigs and quickly pushing black strollers with babies inside.

Danny realized that Shabbat was coming sooner than we thought when he looked up the sunset time on his phone.

"We only have an hour and a half until candle lighting," he said, turning to me.

"Is that bad?" I asked.

He looked down Marcy Avenue. "Yeah, because all the stores are closing. We need to hurry."

We saw a Hasidic man getting into his minivan.

"Excuse me," Danny said. "We're trying to get to the deli before Shabbat comes in. If we walk, we won't make it there in time."

"Come on," the man said with urgency in his voice.

We hopped into his car. He drove fast down the road and pulled up to a little market.

"Thank you!" we yelled as we ran into the store.

"Have a good Shabbos!" he yelled back.

We got our challah, pre-cooked meat, and wine right on time. We were the last customers in the store. We went home and set the table. When it was time to light the candles at sunset to mark the beginning of Shabbat, Danny told me the blessing line by line. I repeated it in Hebrew, not knowing a word of what I was saying.

"Baruch," he said.

"Baruch," I repeated.

"Atah," he said.

"Atah," I repeated.

And on we went. I covered my eyes as I said the blessing. When I opened them, I looked at the beautiful flames on the candles leaping toward the sky. I then turned to Danny.

"Shabbat Shalom," he said, and kissed my cheek.

"Shabbat Shalom," I repeated, kissing him back.

Suddenly, it felt so calm in our home. The candles illuminated our table, which was set with a white tablecloth, yellow daisies, and silver napkin rings.

Danny made Kiddush, the blessing over the wine. Afterward, over challah, we talked about our future.

"Do you think you'll start going to the class with me?" I asked him.

"Maybe. At least the rabbi is nice," Danny said.

"Yeah. Perhaps Orthodoxy isn't as bad as you thought."

"Or you just don't have enough experience with it yet. It's easy for you. You don't have any baggage. Everything just seems lovely and nice. But it's not always like that. Orthodox people are still people, and they can be jerks too."

"I know you had a bad experience growing up, but don't let it ruin your chance to become more spiritual. It's not Judaism's fault."

He sighed.

"I guess that's true," he said.

"Anyway, now that you're an adult, you can practice however you want. It's your choice. And you can make it great."

"Yeah. Look, let's just eat now. This is really nice."

"It is," I said.

After that, we enjoyed a nice Shabbat dinner. I was hopeful we'd do it again next week. Eventually, perhaps, he'd come to class with me and fall in love with Judaism all over again.

CHAPTER 29

Rabbi Appelbaum began teaching us the laws of kosher food. I discovered that it wasn't enough to eat regular chicken; I had to buy kosher chicken, which was slaughtered in a way that wouldn't hurt the chicken. It had to die instantly and painlessly, or else it wouldn't be kosher.

I also learned that Jews don't eat meat and milk together because they don't mix life and death—like the Egyptians who enslaved them did—and they don't eat aggressive animals because they don't want to be aggressive people.

As an animal lover, I instantly clicked with all these mitzvot, so I slowly gave up non-kosher food. I loved bacon, but it was forbidden—and Danny didn't like to kiss me after I ate it—so that was the first to go. The next was crab, which I grew up eating all the time in Baltimore. I joked that I knew how to crack open a crab before I learned how to walk. But when I went home once to eat crabs with my family, I decided that it was the last time I'd ever do it.

I was hooked on turkey sandwiches from my corner bodega, but I knew those had to go, too. When I visited Danny in Ireland while he was doing a stand-up comedy tour there, I had a tasty fried chicken sandwich in Belfast and decided to stop eating non-kosher chicken on that high note. However, when I got on the plane, I didn't realize I needed to order kosher food in advance, so I ate the regular chicken instead. What a mistake. I guess God heard I was done because I got so sick from that chicken as soon as we landed. After that, I was really done.

Danny saw what I was doing, but he wasn't so into it.

"You can do what you want. I never ate bacon or anything, and I only eat non-kosher chicken, so I'm not changing," he said. "You're being extreme."

"That's fine," I said. "I'm not pressuring you."

"Good."

However, soon after that, his attitude changed. One day he came home frantic.

"Kylie, the weirdest thing just happened," he said. His forehead was sweaty. "I was eating chicken at Whole Foods, and I felt the chicken's soul."

"What? Seriously?"

"Yeah. I could taste its suffering. It was horrible."

"Wow, that's wild."

"Yeah. I'm going to give up non-kosher chicken. I think that was a sign."

"Good for you. I mean, that's really strange, but I guess that was the push you needed."

From that moment, Danny started keeping kosher with chicken and other meat, too. And the following week, while I was in class, Danny walked in.

He came fifteen minutes after the class had already started, in typical Danny fashion. Rabbi Appelbaum smiled when he saw him.

"Welcome, Danny. Come have a seat," he said, patting the chair next to him.

I couldn't believe it. Out of nowhere, he was here. I held his hand the entire time.

ᘓ

After the class was over and everyone left, Danny approached Rabbi Appelbaum.

"Rabbi, can I talk to you for a minute?" he asked.

"Yes, Danny, of course," he said.

We sat across from the rabbi. Danny, who was visibly upset, started ranting.

"Rabbi, you have a very nice class here," he said. "But I am not interested in becoming Orthodox, just so we're clear. I had a horrible experience with it and I'm not coming back."

I felt a knot in my stomach. The rabbi sat there patiently, not breaking eye contact with Danny, and saying "mhm" to acknowledge that he heard what Danny was saying.

"I decided not to be observant anymore after they kicked me out of yeshiva for no good reason in the middle of ninth grade, and I can't go back to it," Danny said. "It messed me up for a long time. I'm not going to conversion classes with Kylie now, and I don't plan to in the future. I didn't want her to do this. I told her she could get a Conservative conversion if she wants, but not an Orthodox one. This is not the life I want."

Danny sat back in his chair. I sat there quietly, picking at my nails out of anxiety. The rabbi looked Danny in the eyes.

"I completely understand everything you're saying, Danny," he said. "And let me just say this: I'm sorry. I'm sorry you were not treated nicely. Nobody deserves that. I'm sorry you didn't have a good experience. It was so horrible, especially because you were a teenager. That's a very vulnerable time in anyone's life, and of course you feel scarred by it. Personally, I grew up Orthodox, and I'm still Orthodox, obviously. I think it's a beautiful lifestyle."

I felt the knot in my stomach start to untangle. Danny listened intently.

"If you don't want to do this, I don't blame you. But I think that maybe, if you come to the conversion classes I hold here and you start trying to pray every day, you will like it. It's different now that you're an adult, and maybe you can have a better experience. You can shape your own relationship with it. But if you never wanted to come back in here, I'd totally understand. If you do ever want to come to the conversion classes, just know our door is always open to you, and we'd gladly welcome you."

Danny sighed.

"OK, well, I guess you have a point. We'll see," he said.

"Either way, I'm happy we met. I hope to see you here again."

I couldn't believe it. The rabbi had seemed to appease Danny, even if it was just a little bit.

When we left the class and got on the bus, Danny was silent. I waited for him to speak.

"I told you I didn't want you to do an Orthodox conversion," he finally said. "It all seems good from the outside, but once you're in it, you won't like it. Trust me."

"Is there any possibility that it's going to be different from what you grew up with?" I asked. "Could you even be open to that possibility?"

"I guess, but I think you're being naïve."

I didn't know what else to say, so I took his hand and squeezed it.

He squeezed back.

CHAPTER 30

While I was becoming more spiritually connected, I felt more and more dysregulated and anxious.

When I first moved in, Blanco was just a friendly neighbor who sometimes blared his music loudly and gave people tattoos in his apartment and smoked a lot of weed. But then, he started becoming violent.

Danny and I had hired a mover to bring in an industrial fridge Danny had purchased for our apartment. While moving it, it got stuck in the hallway, blocking people from getting into their apartments. The mover refused to try and get it into our apartment.

"It's not going to fit, man," he said. "I'm leaving."

"No, you can't!" said Danny. "I paid you."

"Well, screw you, this is ridiculous," he said, walking out the door.

Blanco burst out of his apartment.

"Yo! Get back here. You don't mess with Danny," he said.

"Who the hell are you?" the mover said.

"You don't need to know. You get back here right now and move this fridge."

"No way. I'm leaving. Deal with it yourself."

Blanco ran back into his apartment and came out with a butcher knife.

"Whatchu say to me?" Blanco yelled, swinging the knife.

The mover pulled a knife out of his pants.

"You really want to do this, my friend?"

They started swinging the knives around. The only thing was, the fridge was blocking them, and they couldn't reach each other.

I ran inside our apartment.

"Call 9-1-1!" I screamed at Danny. "They're going to kill each other!"

"Calm down," he said. "They can't get to each other. I'll fix this."

"Blanco! It's fine!" Danny yelled from our apartment. He turned to the mover. "Just give me fifty dollars back. Then go."

"Whatever, man," the mover said, throwing a fifty at Danny. He turned to Blanco. "If I ever see you on the street, you're dead."

With that, he stormed out. I ran to our bed and sobbed.

After Danny calmed Blanco down, he came in to comfort me.

"Shh, it's OK," he said, rubbing my back.

"That was not OK," I cried. "I can't live like this. That was insane. We need to move."

"If we could, I would…but we can't afford to. We'll never find a deal like this."

I sat on the bed, shaking. My eyes were red and puffy. I thought, Danny was right. There were no more rent-controlled apartments left. What were we going to find for twelve hundred dollars a month? Plus, we needed a security deposit, first and last month's rent, and forty times the amount of rent to find a place anywhere in New York City. We were trapped.

Increasingly, I felt the pull to leave. I just didn't know where we were going to go.

I felt comfort in being in synagogue, in going to my class, where we were learning the rules of Shabbat, the Jewish day of rest. It was from sundown Friday to one hour after sundown on Saturday, when we'd see three stars in the night sky.

"We don't drive in cars, get on the subway, ride the bus, or take any form of transportation on Shabbat," Rabbi Appelbaum told us. "We walk to shul."

This would be a problem for Danny and me. We lived forty-five minutes walking distance from our synagogue. Because of the rule that we had to walk to synagogue, it was necessary for the conversion process that we move to a Jewish neighborhood.

In our neighborhood, there were no other religious Jews. There were Italians, Hispanics, and hipsters, but no one we could go to nearby for Shabbat.

The more religious I got, the more out of place I felt in Bushwick. On Saturdays, while everyone else was brunching or going into Manhattan to an art museum, we were going to synagogue. I enjoyed it, but it was still very lonely. As a kid, I went to the movies on Friday nights. I missed that. When I couldn't drive somewhere and no one else around us was celebrating Shabbat, I felt trapped. All the brunch places Danny and I used to go to—well, we couldn't do that anymore. It was not necessarily that I wanted to go; I was just bored and felt isolated.

The other problem was that since our apartment was rent-controlled, we couldn't move anywhere else. It wasn't like we could just pick up and go to Flatbush or another religious neighborhood. I'd lose my connection to The Greenpoint Shul if I did that. We were in a bind.

It became increasingly clear that we couldn't stay in our place, though. Aside from Blanco's violent outburst, we were having financial problems.

One Tuesday morning, Danny received a distressing call from our landlord, Mrs. Tama, a nice older woman who had been good to Danny since he moved in eight years prior. We were standing together in our bedroom when she called. Danny put it on speaker phone.

"Hello, Daniel," Mrs. Tama said.

"Hi, Mrs. Tama. What's up?" Danny said.

"Well, Daniel, I am a bit concerned because you haven't paid your rent in six months."

"What?" he said. "I pay it every single month."

"Yes, Daniel, I thought you did, but we had an issue here. It turned out that Kelly from our office had been stealing from us. She is going to jail. Now, our lawyer said this shouldn't be a worry for you if you paid your rent by check. Did you pay your rent by check?"

"No. I paid in cash, like Kelly told me to."

"Uh-huh. And did you get a receipt for your payments every month?"

"I mean, maybe I have them somewhere. I don't know."

"Oh, my gosh," I whispered to Danny. "What is going on?"

"OK. I see. Well, you will need to come up with two thousand dollars within five days if you want to stay," Mrs. Tama said. "And then we can just add the rest on top of your rent every month. You can add five hundred dollars to every month until it's paid off. And if you ever find the receipts, we will give you back the money."

I paced around the apartment, biting my nails.

"Mrs. Tama, I'll get that money to you," Danny said.

"OK, thank you, Daniel."

As soon as Danny hung up, I ran over to him.

"What are we going to do? This is awful. I can't believe this is happening."

"I don't know," he said, staring off into the distance.

"But you said you could get her the two thousand dollars. Are you going to borrow it from someone?"

"I could ask some friends, I guess. Maybe they'll lend me the money. I can't believe this."

"Danny, you didn't think to keep the receipts?"

"I mean, I'm sure I didn't throw them out...I just don't know where they are...." He trailed off.

"We're going to lose our apartment. We're going to lose it."

My face was hot. The tears were coming quickly.

"Kylie, calm down," Danny said, putting his hands on my shoulders. "We aren't going to lose our place. I'll make sure of it. But you have to calm down, please. You aren't making things better."

"How can I be calm? We're in over our heads. This is crazy. What are we going to do? How can we afford the extra five hundred dollars?"

"I don't know, but you can't worry. You have to trust that it'll be fine. You know how we learned to trust in God? You must rely on that right now."

"OK," I said. "I'll try."

I sat down on the bed. Danny came over and rubbed my back.

"We're in this together, and we'll figure things out like we always do."

"I hope so," I said. "God, please protect us. Please make sure everything works out."

"Amen," said Danny.

CHAPTER 31

Danny made phone calls to ten different friends, and three of them loaned us enough money to pay the $2,000. We made the cutoff. Now, we had to pay them back and come up with the extra money every month.

I began working random writing and editing jobs I found on Craigslist. I was also still freelancing at the local paper, the *Greenpoint Gazette,* and we were renting out our living room to strangers on Airbnb. Danny started working as a security guard, taking on random jobs whenever they came in. Within a few months, we were comfortably paying our new rent.

Over the holidays, our Airbnb bookings had picked up, so we finally had some extra money. We decided to get out of the city for New Year's Eve and go to his parents' house in Long Island, since no one was going to be there.

Daddy had just given us my grandfather's 2000 Toyota Camry, so we had some freedom to move about the city and go to Long Island without having to use public transportation. He had left it in his garage for years, piling stuff on top of it.

When he opened the garage, the car was dusty and dirty. It looked like it had died years ago.

"Look at this," he said, picking up a stack of magazines. A Camry key was underneath the pile. "Found the key. Now, let's see if it starts."

He pushed some boxes aside and cracked open the car door. He put the key in the ignition and miraculously, it started.

"It's been five years," Daddy yelled over the sound of the engine. "But it works!"

He paid to get the car fixed up and then handed it off to us one cold December night.

"Thank you, Daddy," I said.

"This is amazing, Stephen," Danny said, hugging him. "Thank you."

Daddy just stood stiff there when Danny hugged him.

"Yeah, we don't really hug in this family," Daddy said, laughing.

"Yeah, we really don't," I said. Danny and I laughed, too.

I felt that New Year's Day was truly a new beginning. I knew something big and wonderful was coming. I couldn't wait to see what the new year had in store.

But when we got home the next morning, we were in for a shock.

We walked into our building and saw blood on the floor, all over our hallway, right in front of our bedroom and front doors.

"What the—?" I said to Danny. "What…what…happened? This looks like a murder scene."

"I don't know. Just get inside," he said, taking my hand and pulling me into our room.

Three hours later, around 2:00 p.m., Blanco woke up and knocked on our door.

"Yo," he said, in a groggy voice, "you got any soda?"

Danny opened the door.

"What happened last night?" he asked.

"Oh, this? Me and my boys just got into a fight. Don't worry about it. Hold on."

Blanco went into his apartment and came back out with a mop and a bottle of Fabuloso. He poured the cleaner on the floor and mopped the hallway until it was clean.

"There you go," he said. "Now, you got a soda?"

Danny handed him a Coke.

"That's what's up, man," Blanco said. "Yo, I have a bad hangover. Imma sleep a little more. Happy New Year, Kylie!"

He went back into his place and slammed the door. Danny sat down next to me.

"We have to get out of here," I said.

"That was pretty crazy, I gotta say," he said. "Blanco has done some insane stuff, but this was bad."

"I'm scared. What if he does that when we're home? Or what if he gets violent with us? First the knife fight, and now this?"

"I know."

"I wish we could move somewhere nicer. Or that he'd leave."

"Yeah, but you know both of those things aren't going to happen, Kylie."

I looked out our bedroom window. It had started to snow. This was the fourth snow of the season. After trudging through deep snow earlier in the month and almost slipping down the stairs of the subway, the last thing I wanted was more snow. I wanted winter to be over already.

And then, I had a thought.

“Why don’t we leave New York for the month and go check out LA? I’ve wanted to live in California since I was a teenager, and I have an aunt and uncle there. Maybe they could put us up.”

“California? I liked Venice Beach when I visited as a kid. But could we afford that?”

“We have a bunch of Airbnb bookings. I could keep writing from there. I don’t need to be here right now. We could check it out and see if it’d be good for your comedy career. Maybe we could move there one day.”

“I don’t know…” Danny said, trailing off.

“Look, I don’t feel safe here right now. The weather is awful. It seems like a good time to go.”

“Well, I want you to feel safe. I’m not just packing up and moving to California because of it though.”

“I never said that. I just want to give it a try.”

Danny sat for a few seconds, pondering the idea.

“Fine,” he said. “First, call your aunt and uncle and see if they’d want to have us. Then we can list our room on Airbnb, too, to try to cover our expenses there. If everything falls into place, then it’s meant to be.”

“Yes, then we’ll know God wants us to do this. We’ll see what happens.”

CHAPTER 32

One month later, we were in LA.

From the moment Danny and I talked about it, everything went smoothly. My aunt and uncle—Daddy's brother and his wife—were going to host us. We found renters. We got the money we needed for the trip. We even found an amazing deal on a rental car for the month.

When my uncle picked us up from the airport in his convertible and we drove down Ventura Boulevard, I felt like I was in a dream. It was seventy-five degrees in the middle of winter. There were palm trees all around me. It looked like a movie. I couldn't believe people could live like this.

I thought, *Why didn't I come to California sooner?*

Danny and I met up with his friend Ralphie May, a famous comedian he had opened for many times on the road. Ralphie urged us to move to LA as soon as possible.

"Look, Danny Lobell," Ralphie said with his Southern drawl, "LA is where it's at, OK? This is where you come to be in movies and TV. That ain't happenin' in New York. So if you come out here, Imma take you out on the road with me, and maybe I can work out a little job for you when we're in town. How's that sound?"

"That'd be great," Danny said. "Thank you, Ralphie."

"Now all you gotta do is move here. I'll look forward to seeing you soon."

Danny and I spent the month going to Malibu, meeting up with his comedian friends including Matty Goldberg, and exploring Pico-Robertson, the Jewish community.

As soon as we drove into Pico, I had a good feeling. The streets, lined with palm trees, were also filled with Jewish restaurants and shops and people. It was starkly different from Bushwick, where there wasn't a single visibly Jewish person in sight.

Danny and I went to Mexikosher, a kosher Mexican restaurant, and loved the burritos. We stepped into Judaica shops and had Friday night dinner with a nice married couple. They encouraged us to move.

"You'll love it here," the husband told us. "The people are nice, the weather is amazing, and there are so many synagogues to choose from. Everyone finds their place here."

I was excited about the prospect of coming out to LA and, especially, living in a Jewish community. Danny and I considered it and looked at a few places for rent in Pico to see how much it would cost if we wanted to move there one day. The apartments were much cheaper and nicer than the ones in New York City.

When we went home to Brooklyn at the end of the month, I was convinced we'd move to Los Angeles in a year or so.

Perhaps when we were done paying back Mrs. Tama, we could leave.

I didn't know it yet, but it was going to happen much, much quicker than that.

❧

As soon as we came back from LA, Blanco started smoking crack. Then, he stopped paying his $400 monthly rent, and Mrs. Tama was taking him to court to evict him.

One night, at 3:00 a.m., he barged into our apartment building and banged on our bedroom door.

"Danny! Kylie! You in there?" he yelled.

I woke up startled and looked at Danny, terrified.

"Yo! Open up!" Blanco slammed his fists on our door. "If you don't help me keep my place, Imma mess you up. You hear me? You *hear me?*" he screamed.

He gave one loud kick to our door, then stomped away and slammed his front door.

I was so terrified that I couldn't fall back asleep until 6:00 a.m.

The next day, Blanco woke up late and approached Danny.

"Yo, Danny, last night I was on crack," he said. "I didn't mean nothin'."

"OK," Danny said. "Don't do it again."

But of course, it did happen again a few nights later—at two in the morning this time. Blanco stood outside our door and talked in a normal tone of voice.

"Danny and Kylie, if you don't help me, it's gonna be trouble for you," he said, in a menacing tone. Then he screamed, "You got it?" and hit our door.

After Blanco went home and fell asleep, I told Danny I'd had enough.

"We have to move. Between our rent money being stolen and now this, I can't take it anymore."

"I know, I know. Let's look into it," he said.

"I have looked into it, Danny. I've searched for places. We need to make forty times our rent and have first month's rent, last month's rent, and a security deposit. Do you know how hard it is to find somewhere in New York that's rent-controlled?"

"Yeah."

"We're stuck. We have nowhere to go. I think we should go to LA."

"I know you're upset. Blanco has been really bad lately. But we don't need to make any rash decisions."

"It's not going to get better. And you know how long it takes to evict someone? Anyway, I don't like New York. It's never been great for me. It's too much. My anxiety is out of control here. It's too hard to make it here. Life doesn't have to be this hard, Danny."

"Kylie, I know. Everything you're saying is right. But I was born here. I grew up here. I can't just leave."

"Why not?"

"New York is my home."

"Well, your home looks like it's trying to get rid of you. Think about it, Danny. It's been hard for us to make a living. Our rent got stolen. Blanco is threatening us. And Ralphie offered you a job. He told you that if you came to LA, you could make it out there. He straight up said that."

"That's true."

"Do you need a clearer sign from God? I see it. I see it so clearly, Danny."

"I'll think about it," Danny said. "Just give me some time."

"I don't think we have that much time. I don't want to wait around to see what happens with Blanco."

"Don't worry, Kylie."

I knew I should have listened to Danny, but I couldn't help but worry.

I was still going to my conversion classes and continuing to learn about how to observe Shabbat and keep kosher and how to pray from the prayerbook, called a *siddur.* I discovered that women didn't have the same obligation to pray that men did.

Traditionally, women were often too busy taking care of children to set aside a significant amount of time to pray every day. I also learned that inherently, women were more connected to God. They were much more spiritual—one of the reasons was because they could create life—while men more often gave into their animalistic side. Prayer could keep them connected to God, even when they wanted to stray.

While I'd read some articles that were anti-Orthodox and said that Jewish women were oppressed, I found the opposite to be true. I was very empowered by everything I was learning. After all, kids were Jewish if their mom was Jewish. That was a strong enough statement for me.

My class was a nice break from the real world, from the fact that Blanco was becoming increasingly unhinged and that I was worried about what we'd do. Danny suggested that we talk with Rabbi Appelbaum, who could hopefully offer some help. We called him up one afternoon and told him about our situation.

"That's so difficult," he said in his signature understanding and empathetic tone. "New York is so expensive. It's really tough to move with all of those expenses. Is there any way you'd qualify for public housing?"

"Like Section Eight or something?" I asked.

"Yeah, or a similar program," he said.

"I don't think so."

"Hm, this is a tough one."

For once, I could tell that he was at a loss for ideas and couldn't offer any solutions. It only made me feel more hopeless about our situation.

"Look, hang in there, guys," he said. "I'll keep my ears open for any rentals that become available. And if you need to talk, I'm here for you. Anytime."

"We know, Rabbi, and we appreciate it," Danny said.

I didn't know what we'd do from there.

"What now?" I asked Danny.

"We need to wait it out. Hopefully, things will turn around."

"Please, God."

It was 4:00 a.m. when I heard the banging in the hallway. Blanco was blaring music and screaming.

I shook Danny.

"Huh? What's going on?" he said groggily.

"It's happening again," I said. "I'm calling the cops."

"No way," Danny said. "That'll make it worse."

I got up and looked out the peephole on our door. Blanco was swigging a forty and had a knife in his hand.

I ran back to Danny.

"He's holding a knife," I said.

"Just stay here. Don't make a move."

Blanco started screaming Danny's name. Then, *pound!* One pound after another on our door.

"Danny!" he screamed. "Open up! You betta not let me get evicted, son, or I'll beat your ass. You hear me?"

Blanco banged the door one more time, and I jumped. Danny held me tight.

Then, I heard Blanco go inside his apartment and shut off the music.

"I'm done," I whispered to Danny, crying.

"OK," Danny said. "We'll leave as soon as we can. We'll figure it out. Together."

"Thank you," I said, hugging him tightly.

CHAPTER 33

The next day, I stayed inside. I hadn't left our place all morning because I was scared I'd run into Blanco. It was already noon, and he hadn't come out. Danny had gone to work a security job, and we didn't have any renters at the time, so I was alone.

I cleaned our apartment for hours and hours and picked out what we'd leave and what we'd keep. Danny and I decided that we'd keep our place as long as possible and rent it out to long-term subletters. We had to make the place look nice for whoever was going to rent it.

I cleaned under the bed, in the armoire, in the drawers in Danny's desk, and in the living room. Then, I focused my attention on the storage part of a fish tank Danny had bought years prior but never used. He'd planned to one day fill it with salt water and get a puffer fish, but he found out it was too expensive. So he filled the large storage area with random stuff.

I took out his folders with old papers in them, creased photographs, random trophies from when he was a kid, and some comic books. His stuff was covered in dust, and I began sneezing. I got the trash bag and sorted his mementos from the garbage.

Then, I came across a small piece of paper and opened it. It looked like a receipt.

It said, "October 2011: Rent paid by Daniel Lobell, $1,200. Signed, Tama Property Management."

"Oh, my gosh," I said out loud.

Next to that piece of paper was another one. I opened it up. "August 2011: Rent paid by Daniel Lobell, $1,200. Signed, Tama Property Management."

I kept digging and found another receipt. And then another. I counted several months' worth of receipts.

They equaled the exact amount we had owed Mrs. Tama. Here was the proof that we had paid the rent.

We'd already paid the extra rent by that point, which meant that as soon as we gave Mrs. Tama these receipts, she'd owe us everything back.

I found my phone and called Danny. He picked up immediately.

"I found the receipts," I said.

"What receipts?" he asked.

"The rent receipts. Mrs. Tama owes us all our money back."

"No way. You're kidding me."

"I am one hundred percent not kidding you."

"Kylie, that's incredible. You're amazing. How did you find them?"

"You stored them in the bottom of the fish tank, you dummy."

"See! I told you I had them. I knew it."

"Hey, I never doubted you. You know what this means?"

"What?"

"Now we have the money to move to LA. Look how God set this up for us. It's perfect. It's so perfect, Danny."

"Oh boy. I guess you're right."

"Of course I'm right."

"I can't believe this."

"Neither can I."

"We're really leaving, huh?"

"Yes. We really are."

When Danny got home from work that day, he called Mrs. Tama and told her about the receipts. She stayed true to her word, and within a day, she had cut us a check for the money back. We now had enough money to leave.

Danny then told Ralphie that we were coming out there.

"That's awesome," Ralphie said. "It's so soon. You really took my advice to heart, Danny boy."

"Yeah, Ralphie," he said, laughing. "I trust you."

"Here's what Imma do for you. Why don't you produce this new podcast my wife and I want to do together?"

"That sounds great."

"Alright, the job is yours. See you soon, man."

Everything was working out just like I'd hoped.

We told our families about our plans, and Danny's mom held a farewell Shabbat dinner for us. We enjoyed her delicious chicken soup and laughed with the entire family and said our farewells after Shabbat was over. Danny's mom gave us big hugs and packed us food for the road.

"Please send me the addresses where you'll be staying along the way," she told us. "And get AAA. You don't want to get a flat tire in the middle of nowhere. It's very dangerous."

"Yes, we will," Danny said.

"I'll make sure we call and text every day," I said.

"We'll miss you both here," his mom said. "But this is exciting for you. I know you'll have many great adventures ahead."

CHAPTER 34

We left in the middle of the night so Blanco wouldn't see what we were doing. We didn't want some big confrontation.

We packed our 2000 Toyota Camry with as much stuff as we could fit in it and put Juno and another dog we'd gotten together, a Boston Terrier named Bayo, in the backseat. We'd found renters to take over our place for a few months and had rented out a place in Florida, that we'd found on Craigslist.

Danny said we needed a buffer between New York and Los Angeles, so we chose Florida, a place we both liked. While we wanted to stay somewhere like Miami, all we could afford was a place in a tiny town called St. Cloud, which was near Disney. The room was $600 for three weeks, which was in line with our budget.

After a full day of driving down the coast from New York, we arrived in Florida. I felt the dark cloud lifting off me already. We were living in the upstairs of a cute little house on a lake. There was a pool in the back and long-necked birds roaming around the nearby field.

For the next few weeks, our dogs chased those birds and swam in the lake. We went river boating and to a Chabad house in Orlando for Friday night dinner. We watched *Everybody Loves Raymond* every night and sat on the porch in rocking chairs, where Danny lit up cigars and talked about our dreams of living in Los Angeles.

"Danny, do you think you'll make it out there?" I asked him.

"I don't know, Kylie," he said. "Maybe. Maybe not. Show business is kinda crazy. I'm just excited to be going out there with you."

"Yeah? You're excited now?"

"I mean, I'm sure I'll miss New York, but I'm hopeful about it. And I think your writing career is going to take off out there."

"That'd be nice," I said, looking up at the starry sky.

It was a blissful three weeks in Florida, and Danny was right: it was a great buffer, too. I was ready to head to California. I was refreshed.

At the end of the month, we took the 10 West and arrived in Los Angeles in five days. We were just in time for Danny to perform that Friday night at the Improv, opening for Ralphie.

The room was filled to the brim. I sat in the audience, looking around at everyone as they laughed loudly at Danny's jokes. He got a huge round of applause when he was finished with his set, and then Ralphie killed it.

I couldn't believe Danny was performing at one of the biggest, most legendary comedy clubs in Los Angeles. I knew that from here, he'd only keep going up. Pretty soon, he'd be like Ralphie, touring around, playing for thousands of people in theaters and getting the chance to live out his dream.

After the shows, a big Beverly Hills management group wanted to meet with Danny.

I was confident he was going to get signed and be the next big comedian. Everything was happening just like we'd hope.

Like God planned.

Danny started producing Ralphie and his wife Lahna's podcast, and they hired me to do publicity for it.

However, some issues started coming up at the job. While Ralphie was supportive to Danny and paid him generously when Danny opened for him on the road, he was skeptical about our growing religious observance—specifically, that we were keeping kosher and that Danny was considering not performing on Friday nights or Jewish holidays anymore.

"Look, Danny," Ralphie said one day during a podcast recording. "When you want to be a stand-up, you have to sacrifice everything for it. Even your religion. There were so many times I performed on Christmas and wasn't able to be with my family. Now, you're talking about keeping kosher. That's expensive, dude. That kosher meat is pricey. You can't afford to eat like that now. You gotta grind. Eat some McDonald's. You don't gotta do all this observance stuff. Look at Lahna. She's Jewish, and she doesn't. What's it gonna be, Danny?"

"I'll think about it," Danny said. "You make some good points."

When Danny and I got in the car together after the recording was over, I asked him what he thought about what Ralphie said.

"Kosher food *is* expensive," Danny said. "But I don't feel right eating non-kosher meat. I don't think I should perform on Shabbat or the holidays anymore. I'll have to make it work somehow."

But that was already proving to be difficult.

One week, Ralphie brought Danny along to the Brea Improv, where they'd be performing on Friday and Saturday night. We stayed in a hotel nearby so that Danny could walk to the gig.

Before the show, we ate Friday night dinner in our room. We set up on the small hotel table and heated up our food on our hot plate.

"This is nice," I said to Danny. "It's kinda fun."

"Yeah, it is nice," he said.

After we finished, we walked over to the venue. The first comedian, a local, was filthy. I was used to filthy comedy—as I'd been to many shows with Danny and heard all sorts of things—but I didn't want to hear this now. Not on a Friday night. It felt wrong.

"Do you like this?" I said, turning to Danny.

"Not really," he whispered in my ear.

"It's kind of hurting my soul."

"I feel the same way."

When Danny went on, he didn't touch the microphone because then he'd technically be breaking Shabbat. Right now, we were only breaking the "spirit" of Shabbat by not celebrating at home. Still, it didn't feel like there was much of a difference to me.

As the night progressed, people got rowdier and drunker. The opening act and some locals invited us to go out to eat with them after the show, but we declined. Instead, we walked back to our room.

"How do you feel? I think you did great tonight," I said to Danny.

"Yeah, I did well, but it just felt weird. I wanted to be home doing Shabbat with you, not performing for a bunch of drunk people."

"I understand."

"How am I going to do comedy like this? I'm not being a good comedian, and I'm not being a good Jew."

"I don't know," I said. "But I have faith you'll figure it out."

A few weeks later, Danny's meeting with the Beverly Hills managers was coming up. He got a haircut, used our credit card to buy a nice new shirt, and arrived at the office confident.

"Good luck," I said to him as I waited in the lobby. "They'll love you."

I scrolled through my phone for over an hour. What was taking so long?

Then, I thought, this is probably a good thing. The managers were likely interested in him.

Danny came out of the meeting smiling.

"I'll see you soon," he said to the manager, who was still in the room. Then he came walking down the hallway. "Let's go," he told me, taking my hand.

In the elevator, I finally asked him.

"So how did it go?"

"It was great," he said. "He really liked me. We're going to have another meeting soon. He said he's going to follow up this week."

"That's amazing!" I said, hugging Danny. "Congrats. I knew everything would work out."

Soon after, the manager took Danny out for drinks at an Irish bar nearby. They talked for hours, and Danny came home encouraged.

"I think they're going to sign me," he said.

"Wow," I said. "You know, I'm sure they will. And then you'll get to tour and be on TV and in movies. It's all happening for you. I'm so proud of you."

"Thank you," Danny said, kissing my forehead.

CHAPTER 35

Days went by, and Danny heard nothing from the managers.

He waited patiently for them to call him. When he wasn't working with Ralphie, he'd sit on the couch, scrolling on his phone, hoping the call would come in. At the end of each day, when it hadn't, I'd check in with him.

"Are you OK? I'm sure they'll call," I said on day three.

"It's doubtful," he said.

"Why?"

"Because it just isn't going to work out for me. They wouldn't be taking this long if they wanted to work with me."

"You don't know what's going on with them. Maybe they're super busy right now. Don't give up hope."

After a week, I told Danny to call the manager and see what was going on.

"That's going to look pathetic," he told me.

"No, it won't. It'll show that you're persistent. They'll like it."

"OK. But it's not going to turn out well."

He dialed the number. Somebody answered. I smiled and gave him an encouraging thumbs up.

"Uh-huh," he said. "No, yeah. Of course. I understand. OK. Thanks so much."

"So what happened?" I said.

"They said I wasn't the right fit. They don't know what to do with me."

"What does that mean?"

"I don't know."

"What? You can podcast. You can do stand-up. You can do characters. What do you mean, they don't know what to do with you? You're hilarious."

"That's what they said," Danny said, staring at the floor.

"Seriously? Well, they're stupid. You can't let this get you down. Try another manager."

"How?"

"I'm not sure."

"Well, maybe you could manage me."

"What do you mean?"

"You were great as the booker on *Comical Radio.* I bet you could book me on shows. I bet you could get me some work."

"I don't think so. I'm not a manager."

"So? Everyone fakes it 'til they make it in this business. Just give it a try, OK?"

"Fine, I'll try. I'll try to get you on some podcasts."

I started reaching out to all the comedy podcasts in Los Angeles. Danny had just been on *This American Life,* the number one radio show, where he told a story about our rooster with Blanco. It had aired before things with Blanco turned sour. I figured I could use the leverage to get Danny more appearances.

After about a week, the requests came in; I had booked Danny on nine podcasts. We drove to different parts of LA together, and he appeared on people's podcasts in their studios and homes. Danny was having a blast. His mood completely changed.

"Thanks for helping me, Kylie," he said to me in the car one night as we were coming home. "I was pretty hopeless. Things are looking up."

"See? I told you," I said as I held his hand.

As Danny began to feel more confident in himself, he decided to call his friends with big podcasts. One of them was Marc Maron, whose podcast *WTF* was the most popular comedy show at the time.

On a Tuesday morning, Danny came into the living room, where I was working on my laptop, and gave me a hug.

"Marc's going to have me on," he said.

"Are you for real?" I said. "This is huge, Danny."

"I know."

"I can't wait. Can I come?"

"Sure. It'll be fun."

The day of Danny's appearance, as we made the hour-long drive to Highland Park, we started talking about my conversion and what we wanted our future to look like.

"So," I said, "do you think if we get married and have kids, we'll send them to Jewish school?"

"I don't know," Danny said. "I'm not even ready to think about marriage. But the Jewish school system messed me up. And it's too expensive."

"Danny, we've been together for three years now. You don't think about our future?"

"No. Let's take it one day at a time."

"But why don't you think about marriage? I mean, I want us to be shomer Shabbat and have kids and send them to Jewish schools. It seems like the best thing to do."

"Maybe. I don't know."

"You like praying, right?"

"Yes."

"OK. So what's the big deal? It seems like we're just naturally going to become more religious and hopefully get married. It would be great, don't you think?"

"Look, I don't want to repeat the patterns of my childhood. I don't want to put any children what I went through with my schools. I can't commit to anything right now."

"I just think we should talk about it."

"Not now," he said.

We were silent the rest of the ride there.

When we arrived, Marc and his assistant greeted us. He lived in a very cool, '70s-style home with hardwood floors and records everywhere.

"Want a cup of coffee?" Marc asked me.

"Sure, thank you," I said. I was a bit starstruck because I loved Marc's podcast. And when I got starstruck, I also got quiet.

Marc handed me a cup of coffee with his face and his cat's face on it. I laughed.

"Nice mug," I said.

"Thanks. I think so too," he said. "Let's get back there now, Danny."

"Bye, Danny," I said, waving.

"See you later," he said.

I waited on the couch for two hours. Thankfully, I'd brought my laptop, so I connected to the Wi-Fi and worked on getting Danny on more shows.

After the podcast was over, Marc and Danny came out and got some pictures together.

"That was really good, buddy," Marc told Danny, patting him on the back.

"Thank you so much, Marc," Danny said. "I really appreciate it."

As soon as we got in the car, Danny started breathing heavy.

"How did it go?" I said.

"I don't know. I got all messed up in the head because we were talking about religion right before it. I think I said some negative things about Judaism. I really don't even remember."

"Seriously? Oh no."

"It all went so fast."

"Do you know when it'll be out?"

"He said in two weeks."

"OK. Well, are you happy you did it?"

"I don't think I did that well. We'll see."

Two weeks later, Danny's episode aired. In it, he talked about his struggles with Judaism and his skepticism of religion in general. He was just being honest. I thought it was a great interview. It was funny and deep at the same time, and I told Danny so.

"I can't listen to it," he said. "I sound stupid."

"No, you don't," I said.

After the episode aired, Danny received an email from a big literary agency. They were interested in possibly representing him to write a book about his journey with religion. When we read the email, I gave him a big hug.

"See? It's all happening now!"

"Yeah, I guess my interview wasn't so bad," Danny said.

"Wasn't so bad? It was awesome, Danny. Now, let's get to work."

We worked on an essay for two weeks, staying up late, revising it over and over. I typed for Danny and gave him suggestions. The piece was about how he had stopped being observant for over a decade but was coming back to it because of me.

When we turned it in, the agent took a month to read it. And when she finally emailed us, it wasn't good news.

"This isn't what we were looking for," she wrote. "Can you try to talk more about religion in your childhood?"

"Sure," Danny replied.

We rewrote it, talking about how Danny loved being religious as a child, then moved away from it. But he was coming back around and considering becoming fully observant. The chapter was moving and powerful…or so we thought.

After emailing it in and following up twice, we received an email from the agent five weeks later.

"This just isn't going to work," she told us. "But best of luck selling it elsewhere!"

Danny was defeated.

"Seriously, what did she want from me?" he asked me.

"I'm not sure," I said. "I thought it was great."

"Maybe she wanted me to talk about leaving religion more. Maybe she thought that because I talked about my struggles on Maron, I was becoming less religious?"

"That would make sense. Publishers seem to like juicy stories about people leaving Orthodox Judaism. Becoming religious is not so enticing to them."

"It's so frustrating. I keep trying, but nobody wants me."

"Danny, you can't give up. You're so talented. If someone doesn't want you, they're stupid. Seriously. Idiots. Numbskulls. Dum-dums!"

Danny smiled.

"Thanks," he said. "I love you."

"Love you, too."

The stand-up gigs in LA were not like the ones in New York.

On any given night, when Danny was performing in New York, he could do five shows if he wanted. There were always shows happening and plenty of stage time to go around. He spent years handing out flyers to tourists in the West Village so he could get a few minutes on stage at 3:00 a.m. and perform in front of five drunk people. But he loved it.

In LA, stage time was very hard to come by. There were many more celebrities in LA, and they were the priority, even if they weren't funny. Their faces on a flyer would sell tickets.

I would email ten shows a week and follow up day after day. With all my efforts, I was only able to get him on about a show a week, and it was never that great.

We'd usually have to drive at least an hour to some faraway place. The show would be at an informal venue—a coffee shop or someone's apartment—and there wouldn't be that many people in the audience. We lost gas money and time. After one disappointing gig, Danny was ready to stop trying.

"Don't email anyone else," he said. "It's not worth it."

"For once, I agree with you about this. It's pretty hopeless," I said.

In New York, Danny had a manager and did a Comedy Central showcase and was going somewhere. In LA, he was a nobody. We had to do something different.

CHAPTER 36

I found out about a networking group for women who were comedy managers and agents, and I went to a meet up with them at the Improv, a famous comedy club in LA.

The other women were nice and supportive. A few of them offered to meet with me.

"I suggest you get a job at an agency to try to build your client roster," one of the women told me. "If you want a referral, I'd be happy to help you."

"That would be amazing," I said.

I was writing, but it wasn't exactly paying the bills. If I could get a real job in comedy, perhaps I could help Danny. I still knew in my heart he was going to be famous, and maybe this is how it would happen.

I soon found a listing for an assistant position at a big agency and applied. The woman from the networking group sent in a complimentary note about me, and I snagged an interview. It was so exciting; if I got it, I'd be working for a comedy manager with big-time clients.

The day of my interview, I dressed up in a blazer and did my makeup nicely. When I got to the fancy building the agency had in Beverly Hills, I waited in the lobby for ten minutes before the manager called me in. He had slicked-back hair and was wearing a suit. He must have only been a few years older than me.

He asked me about my experience and my dreams for my career in comedy.

"I helped Ralphie May with his publicity, and I got my husband on a lot of podcasts and comedy shows around town," I said. "I booked a big podcast, *Comical Radio,* and interned at *The Daily Show* and *The Onion.*"

"Wow, that's really impressive," the agent said. "You sound like you'd be a great fit for this job."

Then, he turned to me very seriously.

"Let me ask you this, Kylie. There's just one thing that concerns me. Are you planning to have kids any time soon?"

"Um, uh, no," I said.

"That's good. How about this: Would you work on the weekends?"

The manager was Jewish, so I thought I could be open with him.

"I take off Friday nights and Saturdays for Shabbat, but other than that, I am totally open to working nights and weekends," I said. "I'm a very hard worker."

"Uh-huh," he said. He then stood up quickly. I stood up. He shook my hand.

"I'll be in touch," he said.

He sat back down, and I let myself out. I didn't feel right about the questions he asked me, but I wanted the job so badly that I was willing to take it.

I waited and waited for him to email me, but the message never came. Finally, after two weeks, I emailed him, and he got back to me right away.

"We went with someone else, but thanks for applying!" he said.

That was it. I didn't know what else to do at this point. How could I help Danny? How could I help us? What was our future going to be?

Danny started taking improv classes at The Second City. He went through the entire program and ended up graduating, which looked good on his résumé. Because of this, he finally landed an agent. It was just for commercials, but it was a start.

The agent would send him out on auditions, usually with less than a day's notice. He was driving around town and always hoped to land a gig, but out of the forty or so he went on, he only booked one for $800.

Danny was supposed to be on-call as much as possible, and when he wasn't available, he needed to tell his agents. *Simchat Torah,* which was right at the end of the High Holiday season, fell on a Monday, and Danny forgot to say he wouldn't be available that day. We didn't know; we found out after the holiday when Danny turned on his phone and heard an angry voicemail from his agents.

"Where are you?" a woman on the line said. "Call me now."

That was from the day prior. Danny called her back as soon as he heard it and put it on speaker phone. When she picked up, she didn't even say hello.

"Where have you been?" she said. "We got you an audition."

"It was a Jewish holiday. Simchat Torah," he said.

"That's not a real holiday," she said.

"Yes, it is."

"Look, if you want to make it in this business, you can't take off for a Jewish holiday nobody's ever even heard of. And you certainly can't forget to take off for it. This isn't a good fit. Goodbye."

We were stunned. I looked at Danny.

"I can't believe that," I said. "That's straight up discrimination."

"Yeah, well, that's Hollywood. They're jerks."

"I mean, you messed up not taking off, but they took it to a whole other level."

"They're insane. I don't want them to rep me anymore."

"Sorry that happened."

"It's fine. Maybe I'll find someone else."

A few months later, Danny found another agent. Right away, they sent him a script for a prominent part that paid well. He read me the script. In it, he was supposed to kiss another woman.

"I don't want you doing that," I told him.

"But it's just acting," he said.

"So? You're still kissing another woman. What if you fall in love with her? This is how affairs start."

"Seriously? I think you're being a little crazy."

"No, I'm not. The Torah forbids you to even shake hands with another woman who isn't your wife. Maybe those rules are in place for a reason."

"Well, we aren't married yet. Does it really matter that much?"

I sighed. "I don't care if we aren't married yet. You're not kissing another woman. That's where I draw the line."

"Don't you see how limiting this is? I'm going to have to turn down so many parts if I can't even shake hands with another woman."

"There will be other parts. You don't have to do that."

"It just sucks. What am I going to do?"

I felt for Danny. I didn't want him to be creatively stifled. But I knew that show business was not the best place because we had so many negative experiences in it.

One night, when Danny and I were at the Improv, a famous Jewish comedian came up to us.

"So, how it's going, Rabbi?" he asked Danny, who wasn't wearing a yarmulke or otherwise dressed religious.

Danny laughed. He was noticeably uncomfortable.

"Oh, fine, but I'm not a rabbi," he said.

"And how's your wife, the rebbetzin?" the comedian continued. "She's looking really good tonight."

I laughed nervously.

"Um, she's good. Hey, it's good to see you," Danny said, pulling me away.

"What was that?" I whispered to Danny. "First of all, how does he know you're religious? And why is he making fun of it? And why is he hitting on me?"

"They don't respect me, Kylie. They don't like that I'm religious."

We had invited some comedians and bookers over for Shabbat dinner, and word must have spread that Danny was observant. We were trying to be friendly, to give people an authentic Shabbat experience, something some of them had never done. But it was now working against us.

"That's such BS," I said. "I can't believe this."

"Yeah, well, every door is shutting because I chose this," he said. "There's nothing I can do now."

While Danny was struggling with his career, I got some disappointing news from Rabbi Appelbaum. I learned that I couldn't convert with him anymore because I wasn't living in New York.

I'd called Rabbi Appelbaum to check in with him when he broke the news to me.

"Kylie, I can't keep working with you on your conversion, but I'm here any time you need me," he said. "If you have any questions at all, feel free to reach out. Seriously."

"Thank you, Rabbi Appelbaum," I said, tearing up.

Like Danny, I also had to admit that I felt lost in Los Angeles. It was such a huge place, we didn't know many people, and it was difficult to make friends. It had been several months since we got there, and I didn't really know anyone. I spoke to Anath on the phone sometimes, but that was it. She was in New York; I was 3,000 miles away.

Danny's only friend in LA was Matty Goldberg. We'd see Matty only once every few months because he lived an hour away. Most days, Danny would sit on the couch, scrolling social media and telling me about how all his comedy friends were making it now. His job with Ralphie had ended when he and his wife separated. Now, Danny was aimless, and looking at what other people were doing was getting to him.

"Megan just got a writing job on *Conan,*" he'd say. Or: "Michael's going on a huge stand-up tour."

"Look, you're on a different path," I said. "And you don't know what's going on behind the scenes. Do they have boyfriends or girlfriends? Do they want children? Are they happy? Just because it looks great from the outside, it doesn't mean it is."

"It looks pretty good to me. I want that."

"I think you should stop torturing yourself and put down your phone. Go outside for a walk or something."

"I don't feel like it. I'm so depressed."

I couldn't be inside our apartment. I couldn't be like Danny. When I was a kid, I was bored all the time, and it was awful. I had to stay busy. I'd go out to the gym or the local coffee shop and get some work done. And when I'd come home hours later, Danny would still be on the couch.

"Did you do anything?" I'd say when I got back.

"Nope," he'd say.

"I don't understand why you aren't making content. You can still do your own thing and try to make it."

"I have no motivation. The industry doesn't want me, and they control everything. If Hollywood doesn't want me to make it big, I won't."

"That's not true. What about creating sketches for YouTube? How about writing a new hour of stand-up? Or what about doing another podcast?"

"No one will see my sketches, I won't have anywhere to perform my hour, and my podcast will get, like, five subscribers. Doesn't seem worth it to me. I've tried, Kylie. And I'm tired."

"You never know what will take off."

"Look," Danny said, sighing. "You can't relate. You get to write. Your industry hasn't rejected you. Imagine if you couldn't write anymore. What would you do? Could you just switch to another career? Or would it be very, very painful?"

I thought about it for a second.

"Yeah, I guess you're right," I said. "It would be tough for sure. But I still think that giving up isn't the answer."

"I'm not giving up. I'm just not doing anything right now."

"You're acting like a retired person, though. If you need to get on antidepressants or go to therapy, do it. I can't stand this constant moping around."

"Thanks for being understanding. You're real empathetic."

Danny got up and went outside to lay on the hammock. I left and went back to the coffee shop. I didn't want to be around him.

CHAPTER 37

What kept Danny and me together during those rough moments was knowing that as soon as Shabbat came in, we'd stop fighting. That was our promise to each other. When I lit the Shabbat candles, we didn't argue anymore. We could argue Saturday night when Shabbat was over, but never on Shabbat itself. It always worked.

One Friday evening, after I lit the candles, we were taking a walk on our block when we noticed a huge mezuzah on our neighbor's door. We lived a mile outside of the main Jewish area, Pico-Robertson, since our neighborhood was cheaper. We didn't think there were any other religious Jews around.

"Jews!" Danny exclaimed when he saw the mezuzah. "Let's go meet them."

Danny walked toward their front door.

"Seriously?" I said. "You're just going to knock on a complete stranger's door?"

"Yup," he said.

Danny knocked, and the door swung open.

"Hi!" said a cheery woman in a head covering and apron. "Can I help you?"

"Hey," Danny said. "We just moved here. I'm Danny, and this is my girlfriend, Kylie. We're Jewish too. We live right down the block."

"That's amazing!" the woman said. "My name is Miriam. Menachem?" she said, looking over her shoulder. "We have some new friends here."

Her husband came to the door. He had a beard and was wearing a black hat.

"Hi, guys!" he said. "It's so nice that there are other Jews here now. We thought we were the only ones. I'm Menachem. Where did you guys move here from?"

"New York," I said.

"Oh, nice. Is that where you're from?"

"Danny is from Queens, but I'm originally from Baltimore."

"Baltimore? Me too! That's so cool."

"Wow! I guess we were meant to meet," I said, smiling.

"Well," Miriam said, "we'll just have to have you over sometime. Want to come for Shabbat next week? The kids love to meet new people."

"We'd love to," Danny said.

"Alright," Miriam said. "We can't wait."

We all wished one another Shabbat Shalom.

Meeting Miriam and Menachem could not have come at a better time. We were feeling isolated and alone, and suddenly, we had an invite out of nowhere. I'd soon come to find out that God put us on their block for a very good reason.

❧

The following Shabbat, we all sang the song to welcome in Shabbat, "Shalom Aleichem," at Miriam and Menachem's house. In the middle, Menachem and their little three kids got up and started dancing around the table. He hoisted his two-year-old son on his shoulders, who giggled and bounced up and down. Danny and I laughed and held each other's hands under the table.

Miriam made incredible food that looked and tasted like it was straight out of *Bon Appétit.* Menachem shared some teachings about that week's Torah portion. Danny told funny stories about his life, and the kids and Miriam and Menachem laughed hysterically.

We'd never had so much fun at a Shabbat dinner, and it was the best time we'd had together in a while. When everything seemed to be going wrong with Danny's career, when our relationship was strained, this provided us with some hope. Maybe we could be like Miriam and Menachem one day. Maybe we could be fully observant. Maybe we could also be that happy.

At this point in our religious observance, Danny and I were doing "half-Shabbats." Miriam and Menachem began inviting us for Friday night dinner every week. After going to synagogue on Saturday morning and then eating lunch, we'd watch a movie or drive to a local park to take a walk with our dogs.

It was hard to determine our level of religiosity. Were we Orthodox? Modern Orthodox? Conservadox?

When we did drive on Shabbat, it was stressful. It felt wrong as we were doing it. However, we didn't find a synagogue within walking distance where we fit in, and we didn't have enough friends nearby to fully celebrate Shabbat.

Since we lived in a mostly non-Jewish neighborhood, Shabbat was just another day. Everyone was driving or playing music on their porch or hosting kids' birthday parties with bouncy castles on their lawns. I felt out of place. So many times, I thought, if I weren't doing Shabbat today, I could be out and about and having fun, too.

Still, I didn't want to give up Shabbat. Friday nights were so special and calming. I was a workaholic and welcomed the break from my never-ending to-do list. I knew that if we had more friends, it would be easier to keep it. We just needed to find our footing in our community.

One night, a year after we'd moved to LA, Danny was in a bad mood. He was sitting on the couch, and I was doing work on my computer.

"This place is so depressing," he said. "I don't know why we moved here."

"Well, the weather is great, at least," I said.

"We don't have any friends."

"I know. Only Miriam and Menachem."

"I'm not going to make it as a comedian. Becoming religious messed that up for me."

"Can we stop having this conversation? You're on repeat. Do you post videos on YouTube? Do you pitch yourself to

Jewish organizations to do stand-up comedy? I know we're in a tough spot, but it'll pay off. You'll see."

"Becoming Orthodox has destroyed my career. But I like being religious. That's the hard part. It's been good for me. I like praying. It makes me feel calm. I like learning Torah. It makes me feel better. I just don't like what I had to give up."

"You have to do the work. God will take care of the rest."

"I think I'm done with comedy. I'll just go into real estate. My dad keeps offering to pay for me to take real estate courses."

"That's what you want to do? Real estate? Come on."

"I don't know what else to do. I can't make a living in comedy anymore."

"Don't have a scarcity mentality, Danny."

"You just don't understand."

"I understand that you complain a lot, and you do nothing about it."

"I don't have to take this."

"What? The truth?"

"You're being mean. Do you want to have a big blow-up fight? Is that what you want?"

"Sure, if it gets you to be passionate about something. I can't take this depression anymore. Enough is enough. Stop complaining and get out there. Or stay at home, but don't complain."

"I'm done," he said, storming off to our bedroom and slamming the door behind him.

I followed him.

"Seriously? Just like that? You're stonewalling me?"

I tried to open the door, but he had locked it.

"Real mature, Danny."

I could feel my chest tightening up.

"Danny?" I said.

No answer.

"Danny. Open up. Now!"

Bam! I hit the door.

"Don't ignore me!" I yelled.

It was my childhood all over again. I was being ignored. I knew he heard me, and he chose not to respond. I couldn't take it.

I kept banging on the door and yelling.

"Open up!"

I leaned against the door.

"Talk to me!" I was crying now. "Answer me!"

Suddenly, Danny opened the door holding his luggage, and I fell toward him and caught myself.

"I'm leaving," he said, bolting toward the front door.

"What? Where are you going?"

"To Matty's. I can't be here anymore."

"You can't leave. You can't just end it like that. You can't abandon me."

"Oh, yes, I can. I'm not taking this abuse."

"Abuse? You're the one who's always upset! You think it's easy for me to be around you? I'm not being abusive. I'm trying to motivate you."

"Yeah, well, you're being very mean about it. I'm leaving."

He went for the door, but I pushed it shut.

"You're not leaving," I said, tears trickling out of my eyes. "You can't leave."

"Is this what I have to do?" Danny said. "Is this what I have to do to get some empathy from you? I'm your boyfriend. You're not my life coach. All I want is a little empathy. I want you to understand."

"I understand," I said, crying. "I understand. Just please don't leave."

Danny sighed and sat down on the couch. I sat down on the other end of it.

"If I leave you, will you still convert?" he said.

"What?" I said.

"Are you still going to become Jewish?"

"Yeah," I sniffled. "Why?"

"If I left you, would you stay in LA?"

"I don't think I could. It'd be too hard for me here."

"So, you would go back to Baltimore?"

"No. Maybe Florida or something. Why are you asking me this?"

"Because I want to know that if I break up with you, you'll be OK."

"No, I will not be OK, Danny. I would be far from OK. I would be miserable."

"Then why are you treating me this way?"

"What way? I'm upset with you because you're always depressed and not doing anything about it."

"Do you hear yourself? You're upset with me for being depressed? Don't you think that makes me more depressed? You're supposed to help me feel better."

"You're supposed to help yourself feel better. I don't want to be codependent."

"We depend on each other. Is that such a bad thing? You're supposed to be there for me, and you're not. Maybe if you were, I'd be happier, and I'd get back out there."

"I don't know what to say, Danny. I don't want you to leave. I love you."

"Fine. I won't leave," he said, crossing him arms. "But I'm not happy here, either."

He wouldn't look at me. I wiped the tears off my face.

That night, I couldn't sleep.

CHAPTER 38

Danny was having trouble finding work and getting stand-up gigs, which made him upset. I was anxious about my conversion; I wanted to be Jewish already. We both felt isolated and had trouble making friends inside and outside the Jewish community. We had Miriam and Menachem, but we didn't have a synagogue to go to every week where people knew our name or welcomed us in.

I hadn't been in therapy since I was in New York. After my fight with Danny, I found a therapist to help me cope with my anxiety. I suggested to Danny that he find one too. Our relationship wasn't doing well under the pressure of moving to LA.

"OK," he said. "I'll go, but I don't think it'll help very much."

"It's helped me in the past," I said. "Obviously, you need help for your depression. If you don't like it, you can always quit. But I think you'll benefit from it."

"Fine. If you help me find a therapist, I'll go."

I found a therapist for Danny, and he started going once a week, just like me. Together, we'd go to couples counseling with a sweet Israeli man named Eran. He taught us to state our feelings as opposed to blaming each other and showed us how our past traumas were playing into our relationship now. Finding a common goal—which was to stay together and love one another—was critical.

After a few months, I noticed that when Danny and I came together during candle lighting every Shabbat, where I'd light and wish Danny "Shabbat Shalom," our home was a lot calmer. The blowout fights weren't happening anymore. We'd get into an argument sometimes, but it was never as bad as it had been. Danny didn't threaten to leave again.

At the same time, he began going to some classes at a local *kollel,* a place where Jewish men would learn Torah. This kollel was for *b'aal teshuvas* like Danny, Jews who became observant as adults.

While he was at the kollel, he met Rabbi Elchanan, a red-haired rabbi who was Danny's age. After going to class with the rabbi a few times, he invited us for Shabbat lunch.

"The rabbi invited us over even though he doesn't really know us?" I asked Danny.

"Yeah," he said. "He's really great."

"Wow. But what if we were crazy?"

"Kylie, we are crazy. But he doesn't know that," Danny said, laughing.

"OK, I'll try to hide it," I said, winking.

That Saturday afternoon, we sat down with Rabbi Elchanan, his wife, and their cute little kids. They served a magnificent spread of different kinds of dips, a big bowl of cholent, a bean and meat stew that Jews traditionally eat on Shabbat, and different kinds of chicken and kugel, an Ashkenazi potato dish.

At the table, Rabbi Elchanan taught us about the Torah and recited his favorite Borscht Belt bits and lines from Chris Farley movies. I was surprised that an Orthodox rabbi with a black hat—a marker to show that you were very observant—knew so much about comedy.

During the meal, the topic of my conversion came up. I talked about how I was stuck and didn't know what to do.

"I was all set to convert in New York, and then we moved here," I said. "Now, I'm kind of lost because I can't convert through that rabbinical council anymore."

"Hm, I bet I could help you," Rabbi Elchanan said. "I could sponsor you, and I'm sure my sister would be happy to teach you. You'd need to find a rabbi to convert with, though."

I asked the only convert I knew, Frank, a New York Italian who became an Orthodox Jew, about where to go.

"Go to Rabbi Canick," Frank told me. "He'll do you a solid. He's a great rabbi. One hundred percent Orthodox-certified. Real knowledgeable too. He'll test you, you'll dip in the mikvah, and badda bing, badda boom, you're a Jew."

Frank made it seem so simple. Why was I building this up in my head?

I contacted the rabbi and set up a meeting for the following week. I was hoping I could finally be done with this process. But as I was about to learn, I still had a long way to go.

I walked up to the open apartment door and knocked gently. No answer. I waited and then pulled out my phone. It was 2:00 p.m. I was right on time.

I tried knocking again. No one came to the door. I checked my phone again. 2:03.

I knocked one more time and said, "Hello?"

"Come in," I heard a soft and deep voice say.

Rabbi Canick was sitting at his desk. He had intense blue eyes and a long white beard, which he was stroking. He didn't look up when I walked in. He was studying some book.

He said hello to me under his breath, so low I could barely hear it. He motioned for me to sit down across from him at his desk.

"So," he said, taking a long pause. "Where do we begin?"

I didn't know if he wanted me to answer him. I started picking my nails.

"Um, well, I…"

He cut me off.

"Becoming Jewish is not easy. A lot will be required of you, you know," he said, leaning back in his chair.

"I know," I said. "I'm prepared."

"Well, let's hold on here. Do you live in a Jewish neighborhood?"

"I live only a few minutes from here, a little outside of the community."

"Uh-huh. Are you willing to keep kosher? Will you keep Shabbat?"

"Yes. And yes."

"You'll have to undergo a period of study. It could last a year. But it could last more, depending on when you are ready. You cannot rush it."

"I have time," I said.

"This is not a decision you will make lightly."

"I know."

"Do you understand what you are getting yourself into?"

"Yes. I took conversion classes for several months before coming to LA. I already started my conversion process in New York."

"And what happened?"

"We moved to LA, and I couldn't do my conversion with my rabbi anymore. He told me I needed to restart it out here."

"Mhm. I see."

He sat silently for a moment, stroking his beard once again. Then, he took out a sheet of paper with information on it and slid it across his desk to me.

"When you are ready, there will be a one-hundred-fifty-dollar fee to dip into the mikvah, the ritual bath where you will officially convert. You will need to pay the *beit din* I put together of three observant Jewish men who will test you on the material. There is a processing fee for your paperwork too. All in all, you're looking at around seven hundred dollars total. Plus, you will need to find a teacher to help you learn the material. I don't know what they will charge you. You'll have to work something out with them. Is this OK with you?"

"Yes."

"Fine. Come here again in three weeks, and I will give you the material to study. I will test you periodically on it, and when I believe you have a firm grasp of it, we can talk about going to the mikvah. How does that sound?"

"It sounds good to me."

"Well, then, you will hear from me."

He didn't get up to walk me out, but I gathered that the meeting was over.

"Oh, OK," I said, getting up from my seat. "Thank you."

He nodded and then picked up his book again. I waved an awkward goodbye, walked outside and got into my car. I breathed a huge sigh of relief.

The meeting was a little strange, but not as tough as I thought it would be. Above all else, I was glad to start my conversion again. Finally.

CHAPTER 39

I began learning with Rabbi Elchanan's sister, Sarah, a kind woman in her forties who was also Orthodox. She wore a *tichel* on her head, which I learned was the name they used for a headscarf in Yiddish. Covering her hair meant she was married.

I'd go to her home, which doubled as a synagogue on Shabbat. It was clean and quiet. Everything was in order. I was surprised, since she had eight kids, and many of them were coming in and out when I was there. I thought that if there were a lot of people, it also meant a lot of chaos. I never imagined it would be so serene.

I felt peaceful around Sarah and in her home. She talked in a calming voice and helped me understand complicated concepts.

"How do sins play into Judaism?" I asked.

"In Judaism, we don't focus so much on the afterlife. We do have the concept of an afterlife, and there is a cleansing process for the soul that can be painful depending on what you did in this life. Sinning is wrong because it takes you away from God. It causes a disconnection. When you follow the 613 commandments, you come closer to God. And that is the entire point of us being here: to fulfill our unique mission and become close to God in the process."

Growing up, I felt like there was so much emphasis on the afterlife and now, I was learning that there didn't have to be. What I needed to do was focus on the positive and strengthen my connection with God.

Pretty soon, Rabbi Elchanan opened a branch of the synagogue he was working at near our home, so we finally had somewhere to go consistently on Shabbat. Synagogue started at nine every Saturday morning, but because we were night owls, Danny and I would get there around ten, in the middle of the weekly Torah reading, the *parsha.* At least we'd be on time to hear Rabbi Elchanan speak about the Torah reading, which was my favorite part of the entire service. He would relate what was happening in the Torah to our own lives.

"What can we learn from this whole incident with people collecting the manna Hashem sent and storing it for later?" he said once. "The manna went bad. It was inedible. What we can gather from this is that we need to trust in Hashem that He's going to send us our portion every single day. And He is going to send us double for Shabbat, so we cannot work on Shabbat. Shabbat is what we give over to Hashem. We say, Hashem, I trust in You that You will take care of me. He always will."

These teachings made sense to me. I wanted to be closer to God because I saw that the more I relied on Him, the better I felt.

I would have panic attacks when it was the end of the month and I didn't know where my rent would come from, since I was freelancing at this point. My paychecks were sporadic and sometimes took months to land in my account.

One month, I was obsessively checking my bank account right before the time the rent was due.

"What if we can't pay our rent?" I asked Danny. "What if we get kicked out of our place?"

"Don't stress, Kylie," Danny told me.

"How can I not?"

"Because we've been fine in the past. We'll always be fine if we have each other. And we have God. Just trust in God that it'll be OK."

"This doesn't sound like you. What changed?"

"I don't know. I've been getting more into it lately. Some of the things in Rabbi Elchanan's speeches resonated with me."

"Yeah?"

"Yeah. I like what I'm learning at the kollel. I think I'm going to try to go and pray there in every morning."

"That's amazing, Danny. Wow. I can't believe it."

"I know. I can't either. I never thought I'd want to do that again."

"Well, if it feels good, then keep going."

Finally, it felt like things were coming together. We had our synagogue, and we were getting Shabbat invites from other people. We slowly took on keeping more of Shabbat. The hardest part was not checking my phone, since I was afraid of what I'd miss when it was off. But Danny never had a hard time with it. Again, he'd encourage me to trust in God that everything would be OK whether or not I checked my phone.

Danny and I were also picking up more work. I was writing marketing content for different Fortune 500 companies and getting my personal essays on Judaism into the *Jewish Journal*, our local paper in LA. I profiled other converts in the community and felt so connected to them. They said things like, "I love how Judaism is all about questioning," and, "There are so many rich teachings in Judaism that you can learn and never got bored." These converts made me feel less alone in my journey.

While I was writing, Danny was picking up stand-up gigs here and there and had started performing at comedy festivals around the United States. I'd help him apply and travel with him to places like Arizona and Florida and Louisiana. And one day, he came to me and told me he was starting another podcast. It had been four years since he stopped doing *Comical Radio*, right before we left New York.

"I'm going to do a podcast called *Modern Day Philosophers*, where I discuss philosophy with comedians," he told me.

"That's awesome," I said. "I'm so happy for you. Who are you going to book?"

"I don't know yet, but I think I can get some big guests because of *Comical*."

Danny started booking the show himself, and the biggest comedians came over to our home to record it. *Modern Day Philosophers* jumped in the podcast rankings and was getting several thousand downloads per episode. Danny was fired up again. He was coming back to life.

"I knew you'd be a success," I told him. "You just had to go through the right door God opened for you. As you told me, you just have to believe."

CHAPTER 40

Over the course of a year, I continued studying with Sarah, who taught me how to read basic Hebrew and how to fully observe Shabbat and say the morning prayers.

My favorite part was the silent prayer, the *amidah*, which I recited in synagogue on Shabbat. It was the high point of the prayer service and matched up with the layout of the ancient temple in Jerusalem.

"Our texts say that Jerusalem is the navel of the world," Sarah told me. "It's the place where spirituality comes from and spreads out everywhere else. It's not a coincidence that all the major religions are there."

Sarah had lived in Israel for a long time, working in the tech industry while raising her family.

"What's Israel like?" I asked her.

"Oh, it's just the best place on earth," she said, her eyes lighting up. "There's nothing like it."

"I hope I get to go someday."

"I'm sure you'll find a way."

Danny had been to Israel several times. He spent a year there after high school, going to college at Hebrew University and yeshiva at the same time. I told Danny what Sarah said to me about Israel.

"She's right," Danny said. "It is the best place in the world."

"Then we should go," I said. "How can I convert without knowing what it's like there?"

"I just don't think we can afford it."

"I'll look into it."

Round-trip tickets to Israel were nearly $1,000 each. Plus, we'd have to pay for hotels and food and a rental car—so it seemed like it wasn't going to happen. I kept searching for discounts on flights over the next few months, but the prices never seemed to go down.

Then, Danny brought up how we wanted to go to Israel with one of the local rabbis he knew.

"We can't afford it, but I think it's really important for us to go," he told the rabbi.

"Well, how about going on a subsidized trip?" the rabbi said. "You could go to yeshiva and Kylie could go to seminary, where women learn."

"I didn't think of that."

"Don't worry. I'll give you the information. We'll make it happen, Danny."

A few days later, the rabbi connected us to the yeshiva and seminary, which were part of the same school in Jerusalem. We applied to a three-week program; we'd learn all day, live in the dorms, have meals at school, and be able to explore Jerusalem at night. It was only going to cost us $600 each.

We secured our slots: I was going to fly into Israel on the last night of Hanukkah, and Danny would join me a few days later, when his program started.

I couldn't believe it. I was going to Israel. I was so excited to see what it was like.

It was October of 2014, and Danny and I had been dating for more than four years. We'd talked about marriage here and there, and Danny always told me he wanted to get married after dating for five years. Since I was only twenty-one when we started dating, that was fine with me—I didn't want to get married when I was young anyway.

"In five years from now, we'll either have fallen apart as a relationship and we'll know we never should have gotten married, or, if we're still happy together, then it's plausible to think we'll always be happy together," he had told me back in June of 2010, when we first got together.

One day, before we went to Israel, he brought up the topic of marriage.

"It's been almost five years since we've been together," he said.

"Yes," I said, knowing full well where this was going.

"So…"

"Do you think you're finally ready?" I said, laughing. "I've been waiting for you, you know."

"I think I am."

"You think you are? Come on. You're thirty-one years old. You're getting up there, buddy."

"It's just scary. I want it to work out. Your parents got divorced. Aren't you scared?"

"No, I'm not my parents. Anyway, you take it one day at a time. We're basically married anyway. I don't see what the big deal is."

"Wow, you're so practical and unemotional about it."

"I'm not. I just know it's inevitable. When we first met, I knew it was true love. This is what's meant to be. All we need to do is make it official."

"Well…" He paused. "If I were to propose to you, what kind of ring would you want?"

I thought about it for a minute.

"Just get me something nice. Don't spend a lot of money. Maybe my birthstone or something. I don't want a regular diamond. I think they're boring. Something blue would be cool."

"So, I don't have to spend a year's worth of paychecks on your ring?"

"No. Don't waste your money on it. It's just a ring."

"You're so casual about all this."

"You're lucky," I said, putting my arms around him. "I'm easy. Except for, you know, converting to Judaism and becoming Orthodox and dragging you to the other side of the country in the process."

We both laughed.

"A birthstone it is," he said.

When Black Friday rolled around a month later, Danny went to the mall. He brought home a little jewelry box and placed it in his jacket pocket. I saw it. Though I was tempted to open it, I knew I shouldn't.

I had waited nearly five years. It was going to happen soon. I didn't know when, but I could wait a little longer.

A few weeks later, I took my flight to Israel. Danny's program was starting later, so he booked a different flight.

When I arrived, I had to stand in a long security line just to enter the country. It took me nearly an hour to get through, and when I did, the security agents, who thankfully spoke English, checked my passport three times before letting me in.

I stood at my terminal outside the airport and saw the bus the seminary arranged to pick me up. It was nighttime when I landed, and it was also the last night of Hanukkah and Christmas Eve. It was so quiet on the streets, though my bus driver still drove fast and jammed hard on the brakes at every intersection.

I knew we got to Jerusalem when I saw the large stone walls I recognized in pictures. There were lit-up Stars of David and Christmas trees all around us. The lights, in combination with the ancient walls, looked so beautiful.

Since my flight had been delayed, I got to my dorm room in Jerusalem, which was at an apartment in a neighborhood outside of the Old City, around 1:00 a.m. It was a chilly forty-five degrees outside.

My counselor, called a *madricha*, wasn't answering her phone. I stood outside the apartment and saw an old plastic bowl full of cholent sitting on the porch and a cat approaching it.

I kept calling and calling my madricha. I texted, too. I was getting cold and didn't know where I'd go if she didn't answer. I didn't know any conversational Hebrew aside from "Shalom" and "*ma nishma?*" which meant "what's up?"

After ten minutes of standing outside, my counselor finally answered.

"Hello?" a voice whispered on the other end of the line.

"Hi, is this Laura? This is Kylie. I'm here."

"One second."

Two minutes later, Laura, who was squinting her eyes, opened the door to the upstairs apartment.

"Come in," she said.

The apartment was small but cozy. It was sparse, Laura explained, because the other girls hadn't arrived yet.

"Here is where you're sleeping," she said, pointing to a bunk bed. "I'm going back to sleep. Welcome. And goodnight."

"Wait, um, Laura?" I said, pointing to the empty bed. "Where are the sheets?"

"Oh, sorry."

She rummaged through a closet.

"Here's one," she said, handing me a thin blanket.

"Thank you. And where is the shower?"

"It's just down the hall. But it's cold. You'll have to turn on the *dood* to heat it up."

"The dood?"

"Yeah. The *dood shemesh*. I'll show you."

She led me to a little switch outside the bathroom and flicked it.

"In about forty-five minutes, the shower will be warm," she said.

"Oh, wow. OK."

"Yeah, these buildings are super old. That's how it works here. Anyway, goodnight. See you in the morning."

I started quietly unpacking and texted Danny that I had arrived. I was so tired after the twenty-hour journey that I couldn't wait forty-five minutes. I also didn't want to go to bed after being on a dirty plane. I hopped into the shower after twenty minutes, and it was nearly freezing.

"Ouch," I whispered to myself, shivering.

I looked around at the bottles in the shower. One of them said "Natural" and then the rest was in Hebrew. I guessed that this was shampoo and used some to clean my hair.

I dried off and then hopped into bed. With my wet hair, and only one blanket, I was freezing. I got up and searched for some other blankets in the closet but couldn't find anything. I looked in the living room. Nothing. Finally, I took my coat and placed it on top of the blanket. I was still shivering. My teeth were chattering. I tucked my arms into my shirt and curled up into a ball, finally falling asleep at 3:00 a.m.

The next morning, I was alone in the apartment. Laura must have gone out. I guessed the other girls were arriving soon. I didn't have class for a few days, so I decided to wander into the nearby town.

I walked down the hill to where the shops were and passed a bakery called Angel. Its sweet smells filled the air.

I walked a few more steps and found an electronics shop, where I bought converters so I could use my electronics in Israel. I sat and had a coffee at a place called Aroma and then found a grocery store so I could pick up a few things. I had to cook for myself since the seminary wasn't in session yet.

After I found some peanut butter, bread, pasta, and fruit, I took it all to the checkout line. Then, an old lady cut in front of me. It was like I wasn't there. I shrugged it off.

I saw a fancy waffle place and decided to get some breakfast, since I had nothing better to do. When I was in line, a group of people my age cut in front of me. What was happening? I wasn't confident enough to speak up. I also wasn't used to this sort of aggressive behavior. In America, we didn't cut in front of people in line. It happened to me maybe once or twice in my entire life.

When I got home, I showered and then plugged in my hairdryer with my new convertor. As I was blow drying my hair, the plug sparked. I screamed and quickly unplugged it.

I sat down in front of my computer, cold from my still-wet hair. I didn't know if we had heat in the apartment.

I'd picked up what I thought was a seltzer from the market, but when I tasted it, it was sickly sweet. I figured out it was soda and threw the rest away.

I'd never traveled anywhere alone where I didn't know the language. Israelis seemed so aggressive, too. I was going through culture shock. Experiencing it by myself, without Danny there, made me feel isolated.

✥

After spending all day by myself, that night, I finally met one of my dorm mates: Melanie, who was from Florida and a few years younger than me.

"Do you want to go to the Wall?" she asked me. "It's only twenty minutes from here."

"Sure," I said.

We walked to the Old City, passing a bustling market and shops and bakeries selling delicious-smelling *rugelach,* a flaky cookie with a chocolate filling. I noticed how sweet the air smelled wherever I went.

Melanie told me about her journey and why she was in seminary.

"I started going to Chabad for Shabbat when I was in college, and I wanted to learn more," she said.

"Me too!" I said. "That's so funny. I also went to Chabad for Friday night dinners. It was why I decided to convert."

"That's amazing. Yeah, Chabad is great. I had a bat mitzvah but didn't really know about Judaism. Once I went to Chabad, I learned so much. I really felt connected to it. I looked into this program, and now I'm here."

"Wow."

"I really feel connected when I go to the Wall. It's just such an incredible place."

I hadn't learned much about the Wall, or the *Kotel,* as it was called in Hebrew. Sarah taught me that the Temple Mount was where our Temple was supposed to be, but the Wall was still a holy site.

When Melanie and I got to the Old City, we had to take the long way to the Wall because, she explained, we didn't want to pass through the Arab Quarter. There, we could get hurt. There, they didn't like Jews. We walked on stone ground that was still slippery after a recent rainfall. I held onto the walls of the residences along the way for safety.

Just before the Wall, we had to go through security.

"They need to check your bags and make sure you don't have any weapons," Melanie said. "It can get dangerous here."

The guard silently went through our things and then let us in. It was a dark and cold night, but there were hundreds of people praying at the Wall.

"Come on," Melanie whispered.

We got as close to the Wall as we could. There were women in long skirts with their faces buried in their prayer books right in front of the Wall. Some of them were weeping loudly.

I didn't have a prayer book on me, and there weren't any in English. I sat on a black fold-up chair while Melanie walked toward the Wall and prayed.

I noticed two pigeons sitting on greenery that was growing out of the lit-up part of the Wall. On the other side, the men were saying the silent prayer.

It was a beautiful sight and yet…I felt nothing.

How could this be?

I had gone through this whole journey with my conversion, and I didn't feel a thing at our holiest site.

Throughout history, Jews fought so hard to preserve and defend the Wall. I should have felt God's presence. I didn't. Instead, I just felt out of place. I didn't know Hebrew, I wasn't wearing a long skirt, I wasn't really a Jew yet. Who was I to be here?

When Melanie finished, she took a picture of me in front of the Wall. I forced a smile and sent the picture to Danny. The next day, while sitting outside on a bench, waiting for the tram, I called and told him about my distressing experience.

"What?" he said. "That's not good."

"Yeah, I know," I said.

"I don't get it. You're such a spiritual person."

"I don't know," I said, holding back tears. "I just feel so uncomfortable here."

"I don't know what to tell you. I think you need to get some sleep. You're probably just jet-lagged."

"I guess. Right now, I'm going to the market."

"The *shuk*?" Danny said.

"The what?"

"It's called a shuk."

"OK."

"Let me know how it goes. I love you."

"I love you, too," I said.

I wanted to be Jewish. I wanted to be part of the community. I wanted so desperately to feel something at the Wall.

But if I didn't fit in in Israel, what did that mean?

❧

The tram came and dropped me off a few minutes later. I was soon at Machane Yehuda Market, the shuk. I couldn't pronounce it, but I could try to enjoy it.

As I walked through the bustling market, I saw neat, triangular piles of spices and wondered how the vendors kept them in that shape. There was loud Middle Eastern music playing. It had a great beat, and I tapped my foot as I walked. I passed shops selling yarmulkes with Pikachu and American football team logos on them, which reminded me of home. I got delicious fish and chips and snapped a picture of myself eating them and giving a thumbs up and sent it to Danny.

I felt good in this market. I felt a connection. It felt alive. It felt so different from the silence I grew up with. The quiet of Mommy's home because she was always at work. The silence of my suburban neighborhood because nothing happened there. The lack of communication and loneliness.

Here, people were upbeat. They expressed themselves emphatically. They gestured with their hands and gave big hugs and laughed loudly.

I was beginning to feel a connection. A bit of spark. Like I was finding myself more and more.

CHAPTER 41

A week after I arrived in Jerusalem, Danny joined me to study at his yeshiva fifteen minutes away from my dorm. I gave him a big hug when I finally saw him.

"Hello," I said as we embraced outside his dorm.

"Isn't this cool? We're together in Jerusalem," he said.

"It's pretty surreal."

"I missed you so much."

"I missed you too."

Danny kissed me on the forehead.

"Hey, wanna know something?" he said. "They have kosher McDonald's here."

"Are you for real? Let's go!" I said.

We found the nearest McDonald's and ordered the Big American—it turned out to the biggest burger on the menu. We shared it and still had some left over. We also got chicken nuggets—I wanted some, since they reminded me of my childhood.

Whenever I got a fever, Mommy would take me to McDonald's for my favorite "sick" food—chicken nuggets and french fries. We'd bring it home and I'd lie on the couch next to Mommy, eating my food and watching a late-night movie with her until my fever broke.

It was comforting that in some small way, I could be reminded of the happier parts of my childhood, thousands of miles away from home. I didn't have to discard my past; I could bring what I wanted into my new life. I was still my same old self, just a better version of me.

Being in Israel was an important step in forming my Jewish identity, and I was excited about what was to come during the rest of my time there.

During the day, Danny and I would go to class and then meet up for dinner. We'd venture to the Old City and Har Nof, a Haredi neighborhood in Jerusalem, to visit his family friends.

Along with classes, we had special lectures at our schools. One night, my roommate Melissa gave a talk about how she used to be secular and what it meant for her prestigious ballet career in London when she became religious.

She was dressed in her tutu and danced beautifully to some songs for the twenty other girls in the seminary and me. In between her dances, she talked about her life before she was a b'aal teshuva.

"I danced on all the big stages in London," she said. "And then, when I became religious, I couldn't do it anymore because I had to perform on Friday night. Now, I only perform in front of women."

I detected some sadness in Melissa's voice, like she had given up her career for her religion. Like she was on her way, and she'd made it to the top in a very competitive industry, and then because of religion, she could no longer do it.

I thought, *this sounds familiar.* This was what was happening to Danny. I didn't want it to. I wanted him to have a big career as a comedian. I didn't want to take it away from him.

After the presentation, I called Danny and told him what happened.

"Yup, that sounds right," he said. "Maybe I'll get to perform at some Passover programs, but that'll be it. My career is over."

"I don't want it to be over," I said.

"Maybe some miracle will happen, but I'm probably finished," he said.

"And you're OK with it? You sound like you don't care."

"No, I'm not OK with it. But what am I going to do? I'm either all in or all out. I'm not going to try to perform on Friday night. I could make it work, technically, but I don't want to be around a bunch of drunks. I don't want to be on the road when I should be home with you, making Shabbat. And when we have kids, I don't want to be away from my family."

"Yeah, that's important. It would be depressing to be alone in a sleazy hotel room on a Friday night instead of with me. But I don't think you should give up so easily."

"Trust me, I won't. But I'm not going to be able to be a comedian like I was."

I sighed. I didn't know what our future held, but at the very least, I was happy that he was going to put us—and our future kids—first.

The next day, I watched Melissa as she said the afternoon prayers, *mincha*, in our dormitory.

I wanted to ask her about her career. Was she upset that she could only dance in front of women now? Did she feel stifled? Did she feel like she gave up on her dreams, like Danny did?

As she prayed, it didn't seem like she was upset. In fact, she looked very peaceful.

After she finished reading from her book, she closed it, kissed it, and said a silent personal prayer to God. Then, she turned to me and smiled before setting off to her next class.

Danny and I had discussed possibly getting engaged while we were in Israel. But we had been there for a week already, and it wasn't happening.

One night, we went out to dinner with his friend Lieb and his wife. Halfway through the meal, Danny and Lieb got up and left. They were taking forever to come back. I was thinking: Is this it? Is he planning some big thing with Lieb? It didn't make much sense. We were at a mediocre restaurant with two people I had just met. It wasn't so special. But they were taking so long I thought it had to be that.

As I ate my bland shepherd's pie, I thought about how Danny might do it. Maybe he was out buying flowers or balloons or gathering up the waiters to sing a song to me, like they sang "Happy Birthday" to people at Applebee's. Perhaps he was giving Lieb the ring for some elaborate scheme. Who knew?

But after twenty-five minutes of waiting, Danny and Lieb came back and resumed eating. I was dumbfounded. What just happened?

After we said goodbye to Lieb and his wife, I turned to Danny.

"What were you up to at dinner?" I asked.

"What do you mean?"

"Why were you gone for so long?"

"Well, Lieb and I stepped out because he wanted to smoke a cigarette. Then, he just kept lighting them up. And we kept talking. Sorry, I didn't notice the time. Why?"

"I just thought you were going to propose to me tonight."

"Why?"

"You were taking forever. I thought you were planning some big thing with Lieb."

"Oh, no. Sorry."

I wasn't worried, but I was getting antsy. When was it going to happen?

Danny and I walked toward Ben Yehuda Street, the main street in Jerusalem filled with hookah bars, hummus shops, and loud American kids on Birthright trips. When we passed a gift shop, he doubled back and went inside, pointing out a heart-shaped balloon to the cashier.

"This," he said to the cashier, who rung it up.

"Here," Danny said, turning to me. "It says love, *ahava*. I love you."

He handed me the balloon and gave me a kiss. I smiled—it was sweet of Danny—but I wanted to be engaged already. I'd waited long enough.

CHAPTER 42

One cold Tuesday night, it started to snow heavily. This was rare for Jerusalem. The streets were mostly empty, and the stores closed early.

Danny decided it'd be the perfect time to go out.

He called me up and told me to get ready to leave. I put on my boots and a few layers of clothing and said goodbye to my roommates.

"Be careful out there," Melanie told me.

"Yeah, it's slippery," Laura, the madricha, said. "If you're going to the Old City, watch out for the slippery stone."

"I will," I said.

Danny and I hopped on the train, which was going much slower than usual.

"Why did you want to go out tonight? It's freezing," I said, cuddling into him for warmth.

"Because I wanted to see the Kotel in the snow," he said. "I bet it's beautiful."

When we got to the Old City, we slipped and slid down the cobblestone. The bottom of my skirt got soaked as the snow melted on it.

"You still think this was a good idea?" I asked Danny.

"Yes. It's an adventure!" he said. "Here, let's get something to eat."

We walked into a fast-food joint, which was the only restaurant that was open. It was loud and filled with boys from the nearby yeshivas trying to catch a break from the cold. We ordered our burgers and sat down on barstools.

"When you were here for your year-long course, did you ever see the snow?" I asked Danny.

"No," he said. "That's why it was important for me to come tonight. I just knew it would be magical. Don't you think it's magical?"

"Not quite, but the night's not over yet, right?"

After we finished our food, we ventured down to the Wall. We stopped right before the stairs to get down to the Wall itself.

"Let me take a picture of you first," Danny said.

He took out his phone and snapped a photo of me. I smiled as the snowflakes fell on my head.

The area around the Wall was almost completely empty and very quiet. Usually, it was bustling with people. But on this snowy night, no one was around. It was silent.

Danny and I got to a large menorah statue where you could see the Wall from a distance. We looked out onto the scene below us. The Wall looked nice and lit up, with all the fresh snow on the ground in front of it. As usual, white pigeons were cuddling in the cracks.

"Isn't it amazing?" Danny said.

"Yes," I said. "It is amazing."

He took my hand.

"I think you're amazing too," he said.

Danny then reached into his pocket and placed a little box in my hand. I opened it. Inside was a gorgeous blue gemstone ring with diamonds around it.

"Kylie, will you marry me?" he asked.

"Duh," I said, laughing.

He started crying.

"I'm so happy," he said, hugging me.

"Me too."

"You don't want to cry?"

"No, I'm OK. I'm happy!"

"I am too. I'm crying tears of happiness, Kylie. I'm so happy."

We held each other and gazed at the Wall for a few minutes. I buried my face in his warm coat.

"Hey," I said. "Why didn't you get down on one knee?"

"It's wet on the ground. You don't want me to get wet, do you?"

"Oh, gosh."

We laughed.

"I want a do-over," I said.

"No way, that's it. One time only."

"Oh, man."

"Here, let's go down there now. We need to take some pictures."

I held onto his arm tightly as we descended the slippery stairs.

When we got down to the Wall, Danny asked a couple from China if they could take our picture.

"I just proposed to her," he told them. "And she said yes!"

"Congratulations!" the couple said, beaming.

In the picture, our clothes were soaked from all the snow, but we looked happy. A man with a scraggly beard and worn-out black hat came up to us and sang some sweet religious tunes. We handed him a few shekels and then headed to a little area where you could write down your hopes and dreams on a piece of paper. We each filled ours out.

"OK, now it's time to pray," Danny said.

Danny went to the men's side of the Wall, where his roommates were waiting to say mazel tov.

I went over to the women's side and slipped my note into the Wall. I looked around me; no one else was there. It was almost completely silent, and the Wall looked stunning all lit up in the snow.

I felt it. I felt at peace. I felt the power of this place.

I felt God.

"God, please let Danny and me have a happy life together and have wonderful children," I said. "Thank you for sending him to me. Thank you for helping me become Jewish."

I closed my eyes and kissed the Wall, taking in a few moments of this solitude. I walked backward out of respect for the Wall, as was the custom, and I met Danny by the Israeli flag a few steps behind us.

"How was it?" he asked.

"I felt something this time."

"How could you not? You'd have to be a robot not to. Well, at least you'd be *my* robot."

"Once your robot, always your robot."

After saying our prayers, Danny, his roommates, and I went to the King David Hotel to have drinks. The trains weren't running anymore, so we found one of the only cabs that was operating, squeezed into it, and went back to our dorm rooms.

"Goodnight, fiancée," Danny said as I hopped out of the car. He blew me a kiss. I blew him one back.

When I got up to my dorm, my roommates were waiting for me.

"Mazel tov!" they yelled as I walked in.

"We saw on Facebook!" Melissa yelled excitedly.

They all gave me hugs and congratulated me. They'd hung up a little banner that said "Mazel tov!" They brought out cookies and we all ate them together as they asked me every detail about how the engagement happened.

"That's so romantic," Melanie said. "I hope I find a man like Danny someday. He's so sweet."

"Yes, he is," I said.

CHAPTER 43

Danny and I started imagining our wedding: We pictured it on the beach, hopefully in Malibu.

In the meantime, our program in Israel had wrapped up. We spent a few more days touring the country, seeing Tel Aviv, and visiting Danny's family friends in Ra'anana, a city lined with palm trees that reminded me of LA. The more I saw Israel, the more I loved it. The Middle Eastern vibe was so upbeat. Life was happening here. It was chaotic, but mostly in a good way. Some people were rude on the outside, but they would be there for you when you really needed them, like one big family. I thought, *Maybe, one day, I'd like to live here.*

At the end of our trip, as I got on the plane and looked out the window, I started crying.

"What's wrong?" Danny said.

"It's just...I really felt at home here, like my soul was coming home," I said.

"We can always come back and visit."

Danny kissed my forehead, and I snuggled into him, looking at the beautiful engagement ring on my finger.

"I can't wait to marry you," I said.

❧

When Danny and I got back to LA, we started planning the wedding, and I continued to learn with Sarah. The rabbi had given me a practice test, and I had to know about the laws of Shabbat, kosher food, and the holidays. I needed to memorize some blessings in Hebrew, too.

I struggled with a few of the laws of Shabbat because there were so many, but overall, when Sarah tested me, I knew most of the answers.

"I think you'll do great," she said one day, as we were going over the practice test one last time.

"Are you sure? I asked.

"Yes. There's nothing to be nervous about."

"I know. I just want to show that I'm serious."

"I think that at this point, the rabbi knows you're serious. Just go in there with a good attitude. You've got this," she said, smiling and patting me on my arm.

That made me feel better. In just a few weeks—a week before the wedding—I would be officially converting. I wondered what I would feel like.

Would it be this huge, monumental change? I never imagined that once I stepped into that Chabad house, it'd completely transform my life. When I was a twelve-year-old atheist, depressed and in Mommy's house in the suburbs of Baltimore, I never thought I'd one day be a very religious person living in California—let alone a Jew. But I guessed that was how life worked. It was very unexpected. And I thought that I must have done something right to deserve all this.

I was grateful that God was saving me from a life without Him. Without God, I was so lonely, so aimless, so anxious. I still felt those emotions at times, but once I learned gratitude, to be grateful just for waking up every day, things shifted for me.

Before God, when I woke up in a bad mood, my entire day was ruined. After I found God, I was just happy to wake up. I could reverse a bad mood with a little bit of gratitude. It always worked. And it helped with my anxiety and panic attacks.

I was also joining an amazing community. Everyone I met was so warm and welcoming, which I hadn't ever experienced.

Plus, the Jewish people had survived so much antisemitism and hate over the years. They were resilient. They were clearly a miracle.

I was going to focus on all those positive things when converted. If I could communicate them to the rabbi, he'd see I was genuine and that I truly wanted to be a Jew.

CHAPTER 44

We decided to hold our wedding on the Jewish holiday Tu B'Av, which is the Jewish Day of Love where either single Jewish people try to find their match or couples get married. And thanks to our community in Pico-Robertson, the planning process was coming together well.

A man at our synagogue offered to bartend at our wedding for free, a friend picked up tablecloths for us, and another friend made us a *ketubah*, a marriage contract, at a very discounted rate. We were also going to have our *ketubah* read out loud by our friend, a local Chabad rabbi.

Rabbi Elchanan and his wife Sara threw us a lovely engagement party in LA; they invited fifty people and decorated their home and supplied the food, even though they were incredibly busy people with four small children.

I was grateful and amazed that everyone was contributing. It was like I had extended family in LA.

I was enjoying learning about the wedding customs, too. I found out that it was a custom for the bride, the *kallah*, to not see the groom, the *chosson,* for the week before the wedding.

This made sense to me. I knew that week was going to be stressful, and if we could avoid getting together, we could probably also avoid fighting. Danny and I decided that he would move out for the week. We asked Miriam and Menachem if he could stay with them; they said yes.

I learned that I was going to circle Danny seven times underneath the *chuppah*, the wedding canopy, to symbolize that we were forming our own private world together. The chuppah was a metaphor for the new home we'd be creating. Danny's brothers were going to hold up the chuppah, which meant so much to me. I was happy they could be so closely a part of our special day and new life we were building together.

I created booklets so people could understand what customs we were participating in at the wedding. I wanted to show my family that everything had a beautiful meaning behind it and, like all of Judaism, made sense once you really looked into it.

I wasn't nervous about getting married. From the moment I talked to Danny at Matty's comedy show, I felt like I'd known him my entire life. Even though our relationship had been rocky at times, we fought through it. Because of religious Judaism, we worked on ourselves, on our spiritual refinement, and became more mature. We were stronger as individuals—and as a couple. I still had my anxious moments, and Danny still got depressed sometimes, but overall, we were doing much better. I always thought most couples are totally in love and have no issues at first, and then the problems arise later on. Our relationship had started out so hard, and it got better as time went on. I much preferred that.

Soon enough, we were going to be husband and wife. After all these years, it was finally going to happen. I was grateful I had the chance to learn and grow. And now, I was grateful to spend the rest of my life with Danny.

❧

I wasn't as stressed about the wedding as I was about my conversion. I wanted to make sure not only that I passed the test, but also that I could live up to Orthodox Jewish standards.

I was still using my phone on Shabbat, which wasn't allowed. I found it hard to turn it off in case there was some sort of family emergency. I was addicted to social media and checking my email. But a few weeks before the wedding, I got the push I needed to try turning it off.

I wrote an article about my conversion for a women's website, and the article went up on Shabbat. After lunch that Saturday, I turned on my phone and saw hundreds of negative commenters bashing me.

"What is that outfit she's wearing?" someone said.

Another commenter posted, "I was in conversion class with her, and she didn't seem sincere."

Someone else wrote, "So you're Orthodox now? Great. You're oppressed. And you're stupid."

I went to Danny, who had long ago stopped using his phone on Shabbat.

"All these people are hating on me online," I said. "What should I do?"

"Stop looking at your phone on Shabbat," he said. "Then it'll stop."

"Seriously? Come on."

"Yes. If you have to break Shabbat until your conversion, turn the light on and off once. But don't check your phone."

I thought about it. I wanted to not check my phone, but it was so difficult. What was going to happen while I was offline? What if, God forbid, there was an emergency? I expressed these fears to Danny.

"Everything will be OK," he said. "Just try it."

The next Shabbat, nothing happened—no emergencies, no breaking news, no notifications I had to reply to right away. The world was still intact.

Danny was right.

I stopped looking at my phone on Shabbat from there on out, instead tuning into the peace and quiet of the day. It felt like now, I really was celebrating the day of rest.

I pictured one day celebrating Shabbat with Danny and our future children and how important it would be for us to have that time together, disconnected from the outside world. I looked forward to this new chapter: one where I was married, one where I was Jewish, and one where Danny and I could continue to grow together.

CHAPTER 45

It was the week before our wedding. Danny's mom had flown into town to take me to the mikvah, the ritual bath, for my conversion. There, Rabbi Canick would do one last test. I would dip in the water, be given my new Hebrew name, and come out a Jew.

Before that, however, I needed to pick a Hebrew name. Danny suggested I choose a name that was aspirational, that would help me be the new person I wanted to be. Since I was depressed in the past, he suggested that I pick a name that meant happiness or joy. I had always gravitated toward positive people who were warm and had big smiles. I wanted to be like them.

I chose the name Ronit Ora.

My husband's longtime friend, a musician named Seth Glass, suggested I go with Ora, which meant "light."

I loved it. I thought it was perfect because I aspired to be a light in this world. I wanted to bring happiness to people however I could.

I also chose Ronit for my first name. I found descriptions for Ronit that said it meant "joy" and "song."

Ronit was a common Israeli name, and I loved studying at seminary in Israel. Maybe I'd live in Israel one day.

Before I went into the mikvah, the rabbi and the rest of the beit din, two other Shomer Shabbat men, tested me on what I'd learned with Sarah.

I met with them at a local synagogue. They sat at a table, and I sat down in front of them. My leg was shaking; I was nervous that I wouldn't get their questions right.

Rabbi Canick stroked his beard and looked at a piece of paper.

"Ronit Ora, what are some of the laws of Shabbat?" he asked me.

"Well, you can't turn lights on and off, or drive a car, or cook, or use your phone," I said. "Basically, anything having to do with electricity is off limits. You can leave your lights on or set a timer beforehand. You also can't work. You are supposed to have three ritual meals, go to synagogue, spend time with family and friends, and read that week's Torah portion. There are a lot more laws and customs. Would you like me to keep going?"

"No, that's fine," Rabbi Canick said. "What are the three holidays where the Jews would gather in Jerusalem?"

"Passover, Shavuot, and Sukkot."

"And what do we do on Shavuot?"

"We stay up all night learning Torah, we eat dairy foods, and we commemorate the giving of the Torah on Sinai."

"Mhm. Now, can you tell me how long we wait in between eating milk and meat?"

"There's no waiting period if you eat milk and then meat, unless of course you eat hard cheese. Then there is a waiting period. I know Chabad Hasidim wait a half hour between milk and meat. If you want to eat meat and then milk, you wait six or three hours, depending on your custom. If you're Dutch, you wait one hour."

"OK. Anything else?" Rabbi Canick said, motioning to the men next to him.

"Yes," one of the men said. "Why did you decide to convert?"

"Well, I didn't have much meaning in my life. I was an atheist. I was lonely and sad. Once I started going to a Chabad for Friday night dinner, I felt a warmth inside I'd never felt before. It felt like God was there. The more I learned about Judaism, the more I felt like I was finding myself. That this was who I was meant to be. The community is so special, and the Jewish people are so admirable. I would be honored to be part of such a strong people."

The man smiled.

"That's lovely," he said.

Rabbi Canick looked at the other men, and then at me.

"Ronit Ora, you have passed," Rabbi Canick said. "It's time to sign your documents."

I got up and signed a piece of paper. The rabbi stamped it, making my conversion official.

I walked out of the synagogue with a huge smile on my face. I was almost done. All I had to do was go to the mikvah.

ର

I was familiar with the mikvah, but not the one you dip in. I had gone to a *keilim mikvah* before, where you would take your dishes to dip them and make them kosher before you could use them.

On the day I was set to dip for my conversion, Danny's mom handed me a few dishes she'd gotten for the wedding.

"Do you think you could take these in with you?" she asked me.

"You want me to take these dishes in with me when I convert?" I said, laughing.

She paused and laughed.

"You're right. Maybe not."

I thought it would be hilarious that at this momentous time in my life, I would be making a bowl kosher. At least it would make a good story.

I had spent the morning getting ready for the mikvah, which involved taking a bath and making sure I wasn't wearing any makeup or nail polish. I brushed and flossed my teeth and brushed all the knots out of my hair. There couldn't be any "barriers" between the water and me.

Danny's mom drove me to the mikvah, which was only five minutes away.

"Are you nervous?" she asked me.

"Not really," I said. "Hopefully everything will go OK. I don't know how I'd mess up dipping in a little pool."

She laughed.

"I think you'll be just fine."

She waited in the lobby of the mikvah, which had various Jewish magazines and some perfume to spray yourself when you left. Normally, married women came to the mikvah after their menstrual cycle. I learned all about it in my *kallah* (bridal) classes.

They were called the laws of family purity; during the menstrual cycle and seven days after, a woman and her husband did not touch each other, share food, or get intimate with one another. It was a time meant to foster emotional connection and vulnerability.

I was told that the Torah perfectly timed it so a husband and wife would reunite when she was most fertile. The laws were complicated and, at first, sounded completely sexist and outdated.

But the more I learned, the more I saw the genius in it. The logic was that if a husband and wife had access to each other all the time, they wouldn't be excited to get intimate. I'd heard of many couples who simply stopped being intimate with one another as they got older. I didn't want that to happen in our marriage. Judaism made so much sense in many other ways, so I accepted that this would make sense too, once I started practicing it.

The Jewish women I'd met in my community worked, had children, volunteered, and somehow seemed to do everything with a smile on their face. My mother-in-law-to-be was constantly making people gifts, delivering food to those in need, and making huge Shabbat dinners for her family. I wanted to be like her and these other women I'd met. Dipping into the mikvah was the first step.

And I sure was ready.

CHAPTER 46

When I arrived at the mikvah, I showered one more time to make sure I was totally clean. Then, I put on my robe and prepared to immerse myself. I left my private room and entered the mikvah area, where an attendant, an older woman with a long skirt, along with Rabbi Canick, stood nearby. He had a solemn look on his face.

I stepped into the mikvah with my robe on. The water was lukewarm and pleasant. I floated in the water and waited for Rabbi Canick to ask me his questions.

"Kylie, do you renounce all former religions and beliefs?" he said.

"Yes," I said.

"Now, last week, on Shabbat, you could have gone to Venice Beach and ordered a cheeseburger," he said, stroking his beard. "Once you're a Jew, you can't do that anymore. Are you OK with that?"

"Yes. I haven't eaten a cheeseburger in a few years now, actually. And I love Shabbat."

"Very good. As a Jew, will you commit yourself to the 613 mitzvahs in the Torah?"

"Yes."

"And if the Nazis, or some other group that hated Jews, were to attack the Jewish people, would you stay with us? Or would you leave?"

"I would stay. And I would fight."

"Fine. You can dip now."

I lowered my head into the water. I felt the white cotton Costco Kirkland Signature robe I was wearing become very heavy. I spread out my fingers and toes so the water could reach everywhere.

When I came up for air, the rabbi was gone. The mikvah attendant was now standing over me.

"Kosher," she said, indicating to me that I had done it right. I dipped two more times and then emerged from the water.

It was done. I was officially a Jew.

I went back into my private room, changed into my clothes, and put my sopping wet hair into a ponytail. When I came out, Danny's mom hugged me tightly.

"Mazel tov!" she yelled. "Let's go celebrate."

When we got back home, Danny was there to congratulate me as well.

"How did it go?" he asked me.

"Well, funnier than I expected," I said. "He asked me if I wanted to eat a cheeseburger in Venice Beach on Shabbat. It was so oddly specific."

We both laughed.

"I'm glad it was entertaining," Danny said.

"Get together for a picture, you two," Danny's mom said.

Since we were now both Jews, we didn't want to touch each other again until we were married. We took a picture together, making sure to leave some space between us.

"I'm so proud of you," Danny whispered in my ear. "Are you relieved?"

"Yes," I said. "It's finally done. Now, let's go get that cheeseburger."

We laughed.

Danny's mom took us out for lunch, and we talked about the last-minute plans for the wedding.

For so long, I had waited for this moment when I would be Jewish. I no longer felt like I was straddling two worlds. I no longer felt like an observer. I was part of something much bigger than myself. It felt good. It felt right.

I was now the person I was meant to be all along.

CHAPTER 47

Danny was walking out of our home, suitcase in his hand.

"I'll miss you," I said.

"I'll miss you too," he told me.

He was headed to Miriam and Menachem's for the week. This was the last time I'd see him until our wedding. We decided we'd text each other, but no talking on the phone or face-to-face contact.

I had printed out a picture of myself and placed it on the pillow next to his at Miriam and Menachem's house. I was excited for him to find it.

As soon as Danny left, I called Mommy, who wasn't going to make it to our wedding because she didn't get on airplanes due to a tramautic experience years prior.

"Your big day is coming up soon, huh?" she said. "Are you excited?"

"Yeah, of course. But I wish you could come."

"Me too. Sorry I can't be there. But you can come to Baltimore and celebrate afterward. I'm sure it'll be lots of fun."

"It will," I said. "I can't wait."

Right after we hung up, I called Grandma Riggle. She had started experiencing memory loss by that time, so I didn't tell her about my conversion. I didn't really feel like explaining it, and I also didn't want to disappoint her, especially when she was already in her late eighties.

As Grandma Riggle got older, I noticed she was becoming warmer. She said "I love you" to me whenever we spoke, and she enjoyed when Danny and I would come to Baltimore once a year and visit her. She'd give me a tight hug when I left, and I'd cry every time, knowing I wouldn't get to see her for a while.

While I never spoke about my conversion, I did let her know that I was religious—and this made her happy.

"Hi, Grandma. I'm getting married very soon," I told her when I called.

"I know! Your mother told me. That's fantastic," she said.

"I can't wait. It's going to be a fun wedding."

"I'm sure it will be. Hey, are you going to services?"

"I go every week. God is very important to me."

"Oh, that's good. It's good to hear that. You've always impressed me, Kylie. I love ya."

"I love you, too, Grandma," I said, holding back tears. "I'll see you when I'm back home, and we can have a big celebration."

"I'm very much looking forward to that."

&

The night before our wedding, I couldn't sleep because I was so excited to finally see Danny. He'd sent me gifts every single day for the seven days we were apart with a note for each day. The last one said, "One more day! I love you so much! I can't wait to kiss you!"

I fell asleep at three in the morning and got up a few hours later.

I was alone in my house. It was eerily quiet after a week of family members and friends coming in and out every day. I took a deep breath and thought, "This is it. The big day is here."

I drove to the hotel where I was meeting my hair and makeup ladies and my sisters, Danny's brother's girlfriends, and my mother-in-law-to-be.

When I arrived, everyone was there, ready to get their makeup and hair done. They cheered when I walked in the room. Danny's mom came up and kissed me on the cheek.

"Today's the big day, girl," she said. "How do you feel?"

"I'm tired, but ready," I said.

"Not nervous?"

"Nope. What's there to be nervous about?"

"That's right. Nothing! It'll be wonderful," she said and sat back down in her chair with the hairstylist.

Rebecca and Christina, who'd flown in from Baltimore a few days prior, and I hopped into an Uber. We drove through the windy hills of Malibu until we reached the beach. It was a sunny, clear, and warm day. The sun was brightly reflecting off the ocean.

It was perfect.

I sat in a chair on the back patio, and women came up to me for blessings, as was the custom at traditional Jewish weddings. I placed my hands on their heads and gave them blessings for health and happiness.

I had heard that Danny arrived and was in the *tisch* room, where the men were hanging out, eating, drinking, and taking pictures. It was there that Danny, Rabbi Elchanan—who was officiating the wedding—and witnesses would sign our marriage contract, the ketubah. When we were about to walk down the aisle, Danny was going to come out and greet me and then put the veil over my face.

Daddy soon arrived in his tuxedo. It had been several months since I'd last seen him in Baltimore. His hair was grayer than I remembered, but he still had a boyish face.

"So, ah, I'm in a tux," he said. "I haven't been in one of these in a long time."

"It looks good," I said. "Where'd you get it?"

"I picked it up at a thrift store for fifty dollars. Not bad, huh?"

"That's a good deal."

"Sure is. So all the guys are in the other room, huh? They hang out until you're ready to walk down the aisle?"

"Yeah, that's how it's done at Jewish weddings."

"I saw them sign the wedding contract. You know, it makes sense. It's good to do it that way."

"Yeah, I think so. And if you don't understand anything, just take one of these," I said, handing him a brochure I made with all the information about the customs.

"Thanks. I'm going to get something to eat."

I was happy Daddy was there. Even though I didn't see him very much after I moved out of Mommy's house, he'd always made an effort. He gave Danny and me his car when we lived in Brooklyn—the same car that got us to Los Angeles—and gave me recommendations for Jewish movies. I was excited to show him my world, my community, and my customs. I wanted him to be proud of me.

I thought of this as I watched more and more people come inside and greet me. They slowly found their seats, and I started to hear some shuffling inside. Danny's mom ran up to me.

"Danny is coming now. Are you ready?" she asked me.

"Of course," I said.

I sat there and watched as Danny came through with sixty men trailing behind him. He was locking arms with his father. Seth Glass, his musician friend who gave me my Hebrew name, was playing the guitar.

When Danny saw me, he burst into tears.

"What's wrong?" I asked.

"I'm just so happy," he whispered in my ear. "You're so beautiful. I love you."

"I love you, too."

He took the veil and put it over my face.

"You need to stop crying," I said. "Because now I'm crying. And I don't want to ruin my makeup!"

"You're not ruining it," he said.

We paused and looked at our family and friends gathering around us.

"Well, I think we have to walk down the aisle now," I said. "I mean, all these people are here. We probably should."

"Oh, yeah, I think so," Danny said, laughing.

We got up and took our spots. The DJ cued up our music.

Danny's brothers and groomsmen lined up with my bridesmaids. Two by two, they walked down the aisle.

Then, it was Danny's turn. His mom held one arm, and his dad held the other. Danny was still teary-eyed but smiling. When they got to the chuppah, I stepped up. Daddy was at my side. I looked into the crowd and saw all the smiling faces. It was a sunny day, just like I imagined.

I made eye contact with Rebbetzin Miller, the wife of Danny's childhood rabbi, who had flown in from New York with her husband. She gave me a thumbs-up.

I walked down the aisle and to the chuppah, where I circled Danny seven times.

Once I was finished, Menachem and other local rabbis from our community came up and gave us blessings and read our ketubah.

Danny's brothers sang for us—a little bit off-tune at times—and made the crowd laugh. They also held up the chuppah, just like we planned.

I looked out at everyone. People were smiling. I couldn't believe I was standing here at my Jewish wedding on the beach in Malibu. It was surreal. I felt the love all around me.

The ceremony lasted about thirty minutes. And at the end, when it was time to step on the wine glass, it was like I'd seen in all the movies. Danny stepped on it, and the whole crowd yelled, "Mazel tov!"

Then, the DJ blared "Siman Tov u'Mazel Tov," and Danny and I danced down the aisle as our friends and family clapped and cheered and patted us on the back.

Right before we got inside the hall, Rebbetzin Miller pulled me aside and whispered in my ear, "You guys are going to bring *Moshiach*—the messiah!"

Danny and I headed to the *yichud* room, a private room where we could spend a few minutes alone. I heard the music outside. People were still applauding.

"So how does it feel?" I asked Danny.

"It's the best," he said. "How about you?"

"Same. I'm having a blast. We finally did it, huh?"

"Hey, you're the one who wanted to wait so long."

"I know. I don't know why I didn't do it earlier."

"Seriously? Now you say this?"

"Yeah, this is great! I love being married to you."

I laughed and jokingly hit him on the shoulder.

"You're something else," I said.

We sat down and ate some of the finger foods our friends had left us in the room. We'd both been fasting all day, as was the custom, and we knew that if we didn't eat now, we probably wouldn't get to later.

"So how was it with the guys earlier?"

"It was fun. We sang some songs, and our dads hung out together."

"It seems like everyone is having a good time."

"I am."

"Me too. It's the best. I'm so happy to be your wife," I said, leaning into him.

A few minutes later, we emerged from the room. Danny's mom and her friends held up swimming noodles that were in the shape of an arch; Danny's mom had made them for us. I'd never seen these and was so touched by all the handmade details she put into the wedding. There were the noodles, custom yarmulkes, bubbles and candles with our names on it, and sunglasses for our guests.

Danny and I ran under the swim noodles and into the crowd, where we danced the hora with everyone. Our family and friends sat us down in chairs and did funny little skits and danced for us to make us laugh. Later, Danny sang a song in fake Chinese, but everybody believed it was real Chinese. I laughed hysterically while he was up there, pretending like he was some international multilingual superstar. Only we were in on the joke.

At sunset, we cut into our wedding cake, a coconut cake Miriam's mother, whom we lovingly called Bubbe, had made us. It was delicious – hands down the best cake I ever had.

Everyone stayed until late at night, dancing and congratulating us.

As I looked around, I felt so warm and full of love, just like I did back at that Chabad house.

When I was a lonely, depressed child, I never imagined things would turn out this way. One day, I'd be an Orthodox Jew. I'd be pursuing my dream of being a writer and living in California, the place I always wanted to end up, and I'd be married to a wonderful person who loved me for who I was.

I was determined to carry that feeling with me to my new life, to my married life, to my Jewish life.

I didn't know what I did to deserve this. Maybe I went through all that suffering, all those hard times, so that this life could be so much sweeter. God was blessing me in more ways than I ever could have imagined.

And I knew this was just the beginning.

EPILOGUE

It was a balmy summer evening in July of 2022. Danny was in the driver's seat, and our two-year-old daughter Sophia and seven-month-old daughter Ella were in the backseat, giggling to each other. We'd just spent a lovely Shabbat with Sarah, my conversion teacher, and her family, but now we had to rush to make an important meeting.

"Hurry," I said to Danny. "They only have a few minutes before they have to leave for the Valley."

Danny drove faster, passing the famous coffee shop where they filmed so many movies, the massive dollar store where we bought our plates for Passover, the venue where Danny once performed, and the kosher restaurant we loved to frequent.

In two minutes, we were at the LACMA lights, the permanent exhibition outside of the art museum made up of rows of restored streetlamps from the 1920s and 1930s. This was where couples took engagement photos, influencers snapped selfies, and tourists lined up to get their pics.

Our friends, who were visiting from New York, wanted to do the same.

We found the closest parking spot and quickly hopped out of the car, unbuckling Sophia and Ella. I held Ella, my wildly funny baby who made silly faces and laughed loudly when her sister held her, and Danny leaped away with Sophia, our smart and sweet girl who was quick to say "I love you" and give lots of warm kisses and tight hugs.

Up ahead, I saw them. They were standing under the lights, taking photos and smiling. Even though we hadn't seen them since we left New York, they looked exactly the same.

"Hi! You don't age!" I said as I approached Rabbi Maurice Appelbaum and his wife, Rebecca.

"Well, we are certainly older, I promise you," Rabbi Appelbaum said with a laugh. "It's so good to see you both."

I hugged Rebecca, and Rabbi Appelbaum hugged Danny.

"And who are these precious girls?" he said, looking at Sophia and Ella.

"I'm Sophia, and this is my sister Ella. I'm two, and she's a baby," Sophia said, so matter of fact, as always.

"You're both so cute. And did you know you have the best parents in the world?"

"Yah, I know," Sophia said, clutching Danny's leg.

"Let's get some pictures," Danny said.

We asked a tourist to take our picture as Danny and I held up Sophia and Ella. Rabbi Appelbaum and Rebecca stood on either side of us.

"Cheese!" we all said.

"So, are you guys enjoying Pico-Robertson?" Rebecca asked. "I have some cousins there."

"Yes, we love it," I said. "It's such a nice community."

"I'm glad to see you found somewhere great," Rabbi Appelbaum said. "You seem very happy."

"We are," I said, hugging Ella, who giggled.

We took a few selfies with the girls, and then the Appelbaums had to go on their way.

"We're seeing some more family tonight. But it was so nice to catch up," said Rebecca, touching my arm.

"Kylie, Daniel, it's been really amazing to see you," said Rabbi Appelbaum. "You have a beautiful family."

"Thank you, Rabbi," Daniel said. "It was so nice to catch up."

"I'm so happy we got to see you," I said.

We said our goodbyes and walked to our cars. Right before I opened the door for Ella, I turned around, just as Rabbi Appelbaum looked over his shoulder.

We made eye contact. He put his hand on his heart and mouthed, "Kylie," smiling at me.

I smiled back.

ACKNOWLEDGMENTS

I want to first thank Hashem, the Almighty. I am grateful every single day that I found my way back to You and that You led me on this amazing spiritual journey.

Thank you to Daniel, my soulmate, my best friend, and incredible husband and father to our children. You are my biggest supporter and encouraged me to complete this book and tell my story.

Thank you to my children, Sophia, Ella, and Asher, my beautiful babies, my sweethearts who are the absolute center of my world.

Thank you to my family—Mommy, Daddy, Christina, Rebecca—for being there for me, from patiently talking me through labor (Christina), making cute crafts for our kids (Rebecca), and supporting my dreams and ambitions (Mommy and Daddy). And thank you to those we lost. I miss you every single day, Grandma Jane and Grandma Riggle and all our loved ones.

Thank you to my in-laws, Eema (Vivien), Abba (Richard), Josh, Sammy, Yoni, Dana, and Jordana, for welcoming me into your family and your hearts. Eema, I don't know how I could have made our wedding or had our children without your support. You are an amazing role model, and I aspire to be like you. To Grandma Alice, whose strength I so admired, and Grandma Elaine and Grandpa Leo. I miss laughing around the Friday night dinner table with you.

To our friends and those who helped me along the way with my conversion journey: Thank you. Rabbi Maurice Appelbaum, your gentle care and guidance were just what I needed to get started and find my way to Judaism. To Rabbi Shmuly Lein, your warm smile and welcoming personality made me fall in love with Judaism and cemented my everlasting respect and gratitude for Chabad. To Rabbi Elchanan Shoff, you took us in when we first moved to LA and made us feel like family immediately, and I am so appreciative of you, Sara, and your entire mishpacha. To Sarah Lipman, you taught me how to live a fulfilling and meaningful life through the lens of Judaism and you are my superhero. To Rabbi Jason Weiner, for bringing us into the KI community and being a wonderful friend and spiritual leader. To Rabbi Dov and Rebbetzin Geula Newman, for helping us stay connected to Chabad and always being so supportive and welcoming. To the Sephardic Congregation of Long Beach, whose Yom Kippurs and Rosh Hashanahs, with your beautiful Moroccan melodies, struck so deeply in my soul that I knew I was (not so secretly) Sephardic at heart from the get-go. To David Suissa at the Jewish Journal, who gave me an outlet for inspiring my fellow Jews in my weekly columns and giving me the full support to be creative. To our amazing community, Pico-Robertson in Los Angeles, where we found our place in the Jewish world and have thrived spirituality and in so many other ways.

To Murray Weiss, my agent at Catalyst Literary Management, thank you for working tirelessly to find the perfect home for my book. You are the best agent I could have asked for, and I deeply appreciate all the effort you put into making this possible.

Debra Englander, Caitlin Burdette, Adam Bellow, and everyone at Wicked Son, thank you for believing in this book and being such an awesome team to collaborate with on it.

Shira Lankin Sheps: You are a fantastic editor and friend who always made me feel like my story was worth sharing.

Thank you to my friends: Anath, the coolest, fiercest French Israeli I know—and my oldest pal—and Matty Goldberg for accidentally introducing Daniel and me and being a great friend to us both. To our longtime friend and extraordinary babysitter (and best friend to our girls) Genevieve Joy, who always comes equipped with an entertaining story and makes us laugh. To the Shapiros and Bubbe, whose Friday night dinners and holiday meals were the stuff of legend—can you please move back to LA now?! To Deb Fletcher, our angel on earth who is our LA bubbe for our children. To Mayim Bialik, who is always there for me and so many others, as well as a phenomenal role model and voice for the Jewish people.

And from the bottom of my heart, I want to thank our relationship therapist Eran Solomon, of blessed memory, who passed away too early in 2025 at the age of fifty. Because of you, Eran, Daniel and I got married and built a family together. Though you are gone, your beautiful legacy will live on.

ABOUT THE AUTHOR

Author photo by Jonah Light

Kylie Ora Lobell is an award-winning journalist whose work has appeared in *The Washington Post*, *Los Angeles Times*, *The Jewish Journal of Greater Los Angeles*, *Newsweek*, *New York Magazine*, *Time Out*, Aish, Chabad.org, and *Tablet Magazine*.

She is known for her inspirational essays and speeches on Judaism. When she isn't writing articles, she is also a ghostwriter for her clients through her agency KOL Digital Marketing, where she writes op-eds and books and provides publicity services. She lives in Los Angeles with her husband, Daniel, their three beautiful children, and their wonderful pets: two dogs, three chickens, a tortoise, and a cockatiel.